THE MUFFIN MAN CHRONICLES

THE
MUFFIN
MAN
CHRONICLES

RECIPES FOR
ENTREPRENEURIAL
SUCCESS

STEVE MARKS

First Edition 2021
ISBN: 978-1-950843-43-5

Parafine Press
5322 Fleet Avenue
Cleveland, Ohio 44105
www.parafinepress.com
Cover and book design by Meredith Pangrace

From start-up to multiple exits, this book uniquely reveals the trials and tribulations of an entrepreneur building a business. A valuable read for anyone in business or contemplating the journey.

—Mark Smucker
President and Chief Executive Officer,
The J. M. Smucker Company

This honest, firsthand struggle details the unique perspective of an entrepreneur facing real problems as they unfold. Genuinely insightful and comical with many treasured nuggets of business advice.

—Virginia C. Drosos
Chief Executive Officer, Signet Jewelers

An incredible insight into the life of an entrepreneur, with thoughtful perspective on the commitment, adaptability, and passion required for success. A great gut check for any aspiring businessperson with a big idea to help answer the critical questions . . . "Am I right for this life and is it right for me?"

—Kenneth Potrock
President, Disneyland Resort

Entrepreneurs are modern-day superheroes, and this is an original story worth reading. Steve's story is a tale of ambition, opportunism, dealing with adversity, good fortune, and hard work that aspiring entrepreneurs will enjoy reading. This book blends the unique journey of two entrepreneurs with universal lessons and insights that all small business founders and owners can identify with. This isn't a Wall Street success story, it's a Main Street success story—in more ways than one.

—Alex Schneider
Co-Founder, Clover Capital Partners and Adjunct
Professor of Entrepreneurship and Innovation,
the Kellogg School of Management

An honest book that sets forth, in an insightful and engaging fashion, a journey that encompasses the risks, hurdles and joys of entrepreneurism within a hometown ecosystem. The reader can learn much of practical value from this narrative. It should serve as an exemplary book in a business/entrepreneurial curriculum, whether at a high school, college or graduate level.

—Gary Spring
Professor and Director of the Small Entrepreneur
Economic Development (SEED) Legal Clinic,
University of Akron School of Law

To my wife, Jeannine.

Having you as such an integral part of this journey has made the achievements so much more enjoyable and the lows so much more tolerable. Without your love, support, advice, and encouragement, this book would and could not have been written.

And to the current and former employees of Main Street Gourmet.

Harvey and I have had the great pleasure, privilege, and honor to have worked with thousands of employees over the last thirty-four years. We have shared in many triumphs and worked through countless tribulations. We owe all of you a great deal of gratitude for your hard work, dedication, and expertise in making Main Street Gourmet a great place to work and build a career. It has been such a rewarding and valuable experience. Thank you!

TABLE OF CONTENTS

FOREWORD

This is very exciting for me. Not that Steve wrote a book about our company, but that he asked me to write the foreword. The problem is, after reading my literary eloquence, you'll probably wish I had written the book. Steve and I have been friends for almost our entire lives, business partners since we were adults, and now we're more like brothers. We were truly fortunate we found each other and combined our strengths (and mollified our weaknesses) to create and build an amazing company.

The stories and lessons he provides will help guide your journey, whether you're contemplating starting a business, growing your business, or just trying to figure out a difficult problem.

We had lots of help along the way and received many nuggets of golden advice that Steve has also passed on. So please use this book to learn from our mistakes (this is probably not the forum to mention who made more mistakes,* but I'll just let you know I had no spelling errors in my draft of this foreword) and our successful ideas.

On occasion, I get this emotional feeling, thinking back to how we took an idea and turned it into a thriving organization that now has a life of its own. It is a wonderful feeling, and even better that I did it with my "brother."

I wish you all the same success, whether you create your own business or do it with someone you love.

Enjoy the book!

—Harvey Nelson
Co-Founder, Main Street Gourmet

*Author's Note: Harvey sent me this literary masterpiece, spelling the title as "Forward."

INTRODUCTION

What does it *really* take to be an entrepreneur? What skills and experiences are truly necessary? Are those qualities innate or can they be learned? What is it like when your business actually starts rolling? Rather than provide an explicit and definitive explanation of these questions and others, my goal in this book is to share the lessons I have found to be invaluable in my own entrepreneurial journey. Perhaps you will see a reflection of yourself. Perhaps you'll see something familiar that will give you confidence to go in one direction or another. Perhaps you'll see decisions similar to ones you may be facing now. Or perhaps you'll learn lessons about what *not* to do ahead of time. Throughout this book, I have tried to convey my honest emotional state and mindset, and I hope that will help guide you in your pursuit.

I am very grateful that I have had many advisers, mentors, friends, colleagues, and others in my inner circle who cared enough about me, often going out of their way to impart their honesty, wisdom, experience, and knowledge. This generosity was an important building block in my career. It is also an important quality of entrepreneurship. No one who is successful does it alone, and no one deserves full credit. We all owe a debt of gratitude to others.

The privilege of being an entrepreneur is not something to be taken lightly. I sure don't. *The Muffin Man Chronicles* is my effort to give insight and perspective (and maybe a little entertainment) into the journey of the roller-coaster ride that is entrepreneurship. And just maybe, that will help guide or perhaps even kick-start you in the right direction.

AKRON, OHIO

**It's been my belief that learning how
to do something in your hometown is the most
important thing.**

—PETE SEEGER

I was born and raised in Akron, Ohio, and in fact, it is the only place I have ever lived. I have no regrets. I loved, and still love, Akron. At first glance, there isn't anything extraordinary about the city itself. We don't have hordes of young people flocking from all over the world to come here. We aren't typically even the first city that comes to mind when someone thinks of Ohio. There is something special about Akron, though. And no, it's not just because I was born and raised here, but because it has a sense of community that I believe is unique.

Akron is the home of Alcoholics Anonymous. It's where the first practical golf ball, the balloons for the Macy's Day Parade, and the Goodyear Blimp were all first developed. We also boast a stellar list of prominent Akronites that sets us apart (in no particular order):

- John F. Seiberling, longtime United States congressperson and environmentalist.
- Frank Seiberling, innovator and Goodyear cofounder.
- Rita Dove, Pulitzer Prize-winning poet and former poet laureate of the United States.
- Chrissie Hynde, Rock and Roll Hall of Famer and member of the band the Pretenders.

- Mark Mothersbaugh, composer and cofounder of the band Devo and the creator of America's first music video.
- Judith Resnik, pioneer and astronaut.
- Dan Auerbach and Pat Carney, multiple Grammy Award-winning members of the band the Black Keys.
- LeBron James, world-renowned basketball superstar and holder of several NBA championships and MVP titles.
- And unfortunately, Jeffrey Dahmer.

This personally edited version only includes people who made greater Akron their home and not people who were born here and moved out shortly thereafter (for example, Stephen Curry, the basketball player). I only mention Jeffrey Dahmer because I went to high school with him; in fact, we played on the tennis team together. When I name-drop him to others, people always ask me, "What was he like?" or, "Did you know he would become a serial killer?"

Not to make light of an especially heinous serial killer, but go ahead and preorder the sequel to this book, where I'll share his favorite color, his first-serve percentage, and a photo of a tennis ball I am pretty sure he played with.

I am grateful for all the experiences I've had in this city and all the people in the community I've had the pleasure of knowing. Despite living my entire life in Akron, where you're always only two degrees away from just about anybody else, and despite eventually gaining some business notoriety (not that I am claiming to be worthy of the list above), I wound up on the "lost list" of my high school class's thirty-year reunion. In 2007, I remember getting a call at work from a man asking if I was the Steve Marks who graduated from Revere High School in 1977. Instead of answering directly, I asked him, "What detective agency did you use to track me down?" Talk about a humbling experience—he had found me in the phone book, hiding in plain sight!

As a kid, I had always dreamt of having my own business. It was something I thought about throughout my childhood and teenage years. I did all the usual kid jobs, including newspaper routes and lawn-mowing. I even ran a lemonade stand, though my "stand" consisted of going door-to-door with the product. It's hard to turn down an eight-year-old pulling up to your doorstep with a wagon full of lemonade supplies.

One of my earlier, more intriguing ventures involved a small endeavor in elementary school. I was at a restaurant with my family, and the waitress brought my father some mint toothpicks after the meal. I thought that this was cool, but I didn't like mint. If they were some other flavor, that would be something I could really latch on to. Through some rudimentary investigation and experimentation, I found that if you soaked toothpicks in some cinnamon extract, you got a pretty nice product.

I would ride my banana bike to a drugstore at the local mall, buy some potent cinnamon extract, soak the toothpicks overnight, and bring them to school the next day: "Twenty-five for a quarter!" It was an instant hit, and I had trouble keeping up with the demand. One day, when I was purchasing more supply of cinnamon extract, the pharmacist stopped me and said that I would have to bring a parent to purchase it from now on. I really didn't understand why. I guess he thought I was abusing it in some way.

I had to drag my father up to the drugstore for future purchases. I was a popular kid in fourth grade, solely due to my cinnamon toothpick enterprise, and like any fourth grader, I tried to take advantage of it as best I could—for example, with some freebies to the ladies and a few trades with fellow students.

That all came to a screeching halt one day when I was called into the principal's office. Apparently, some parents were complaining that their kids were using their lunch money to purchase cinnamon toothpicks instead of sloppy joes. Imagine that. There was also some mention of kids swallowing toothpicks; evidently, that's dangerous. These issues didn't really resonate with me at the time, but my cinnamon toothpick operation was forced to close, and my popularity soon went back to its natural state. I'm sure this was just another failure that helped prepare me for what was to come in my professional future.

Growing up, I had the good fortune of living next door to Dr. Bernard Dietzer, a management professor at the University of Akron. He and his wife had two daughters who weren't inclined to sports at all, so consequently, I became his honorary son. He perpetually asked me to play catch with him in my backyard. This is where he coached me on how to throw a curveball, sinker, and slider. I'm not sure I ever did it correctly, but we still bonded. I knew he was always looking out for me and my best interests. When it came time to go to college, Dr. Dietzer asked me what major I was planning on pursuing. It was at that moment that I realized I didn't quite understand what a major even was, but I told him there was no doubt—I wanted to study business.

Growing up in a middle-class family, nearly everyone I was exposed to or close with was an entrepreneur, self-employed, or generally ran their own operation. My uncles, grandfathers, and great-grandfathers all either started a business or operated one. Surely there were people in my life who worked as employees in conventional companies, but I don't really remember hearing about them. No disrespect to working as an employee of an organization, but I seemed to gravitate toward my family members who took initiative to oversee something they were passionate about. This inclination stuck with me far past childhood, too. While my dream was always to own my own business, "how to get there" and "what major to choose" were bigger questions that I would have to figure out.

Dr. Dietzer was a management professor, but he told me that I should go into accounting.

"Every business has to have accounting. If you are good at accounting, you can go into any business," he insisted, backing up his claim.

When it was time for me to decide on college, my parents were in the middle of a bitter divorce, and things were very unstable. I wanted to go somewhere that was away from home, but given the turmoil of my family situation, that option just wasn't feasible. I was a bit jealous of most of my friends, most of whom were going away to colleges like Ohio State, Miami University, Tulane, and the University of Arizona. It all sounded very adventurous versus the alternative of staying in Akron and living at home. Essentially, my only option was the University of Akron—still a solid choice. Most of my qualms diffused when Dr. Dietzer assured me I would get an education there that would allow me to do anything and that he would make sure of it. One of my closest friends, Harvey Nelson, also decided to go to the University of Akron. I presume he chose it because he had missed the deadlines for more prestigious schools, but I can't be sure. Harvey had the kind of personality and demeanor that didn't worry too much about anything, including deadlines. His decision, however, allowed him to eventually play a large part in this story.

In the fall of 1977, I started at the University of Akron, and, as somewhat of an homage to Dr. Dietzer, I eventually chose accounting as my major. I enjoyed the required classes and fortunately also excelled in them. I'm not sure if I liked the classes because I did well in them or if I did well in them because I liked the classes—classic chicken versus egg dilemma, I suppose. Harvey and I became roommates. We got up to the typical college hijinks, but that might be another chapter in this book's sequel. Don't worry, though, they're entirely unrelated to any parts about Jeffrey Dahmer.

I'm giving you all this backstory because my daughter, Brady, insisted that I elaborate on my personal history before telling the story of my business. Since she is helping me with the book for free, I want to make sure I recognize and cite her in some fashion. She also thinks that I will mention her glowingly in the book's dedication. I haven't told her yet that this will be the only mention she gets.

So, on to my story . . .

"Going once, going twice . . . sold to the twenty-six-year-old nerd in the back of the room!"

My life dramatically changed with those words. In 1985, I was a CPA in the Akron, Ohio, office of Coopers and Lybrand, what they called at the time a "Big Eight" accounting firm. My father had invited me to meet him for lunch at a sheriff's real estate auction at the courthouse in downtown Akron. Sheriff's real estate auctions are conducted by counties to sell real estate for which the property owner did not pay their real estate tax. I had never been to a sheriff's real estate auction before, but I was immediately intrigued. It's hard to describe the energy in the room, but I would equate it to the same atmosphere as that of a racetrack. You have all the same elements: continuous puffs of smoke filling the air, men chomping on cigars while looking at their programs and discussing with their fellow spectators. As everyone is waiting for the next big long shot, a surge of excitement permeates the room.

As I later learned, these long shots are appropriately named. You will often see land justifiably sell for less than $100. You might see land that is wedged between two other properties with no possible access. You might see land with environmental issues that are so bad that you'll only earn headaches trying to solve them. However, occasionally, there will be a deviation from the typical listings, a genuine gem.

Throughout my youth, my dad would often tell me wild stories of prospectors buying property right next to a business conglomerate for a few hundred dollars and then selling for several hundred thousand dollars only weeks later. When I would hear these stories, I generally chalked them up to bravado, exaggeration, or just plain folklore.

I sat next to my father, munching on a turkey on rye, sitting through listing after listing, when a small parcel eventually came up for bid at 214 S. Main Street—the heart of downtown Akron. I worked just a few blocks away at 50 S. Main Street in a fifteen-story building.

To give the story some perspective, most of downtown Akron in 1985 was a depressed and blighted scene with only a smidgen of viable buildings, most of them occupied by law firms, accounting firms, banks, and other service industries. There wasn't much going on, nor was there any enthusiasm brewing to bolster prospects. The property in question had little interest, and finally, one bidder put forth a bid of $100. No one else seemed interested. The auctioneer spewed forth the usual phrases when a property was about to have a new owner: "Going once, going twice."

For some reason, I chose this moment in time to take heed of Lyndon B. Johnson's sage advice: "Seize the moment."

"$150!" I chimed in.

The previous bidder was somewhat taken aback and threw forth the next increment.

"$200," he said.

I countered, "$250."

Back and forth it went as my competitive juices flowed. As the bidding reached over $1,000, I felt a little more confident in the process and starting using a head nod for my signature bid move instead of the customary hand gesture. I felt some additional exhilaration as I ditched my sandwich and rubbed my hands together, preparing for a fight. To this day, I don't remember anything about my fellow bidder. I don't remember what he looked like or what he sounded like. I do remember the incredulous look on my father's face, though. I was supposed to be a spectator, not a participant or a speculator.

Bidding for your first time on a property you have never seen is generally not the recommended methodology behind these sorts of things. Typically, a potential buyer makes sure their research and investigatory duties are in order before taking such a daring leap. Had I toured the property? Had I initiated soil studies? Had I talked to the previous owner or gotten experts involved? These would have been good questions to ask myself, but I was too immersed in the battle. Either way, all the answers were "No."

The bidding continued for some time, crossing $4,500, when I initiated a tactic that I had once witnessed on one of those old detective shows from the seventies, like *Mannix* or *Matlock*. It was a sophisticated, cunning tactic; I would boldly increase the increments to let my opposition know and understand that I was serious, that I was a player. So it goes in the TV world.

"Five . . . thousand . . . dollars," I slowly belted out.

To my surprise, and probably to the surprise of everyone in

the room, it worked. Maybe my opposition lost interest or maybe he capped his limit, but the next thing I heard was, "Going once, going twice . . . sold to the twenty-six-year-old nerd in the back of the room!"

I would like to imagine that the room erupted into a frenzy of celebration, that the people around me lifted my chair into the air like the hora dance at my bar mitzvah, but they didn't. Nothing, not even a chair shuffling around.

The next property was already up for bid before my dad's lips came back together. My dad, while perplexed, seemed reasonably calm about the situation . . . for the moment. In retrospect, this was probably comparable to my wrecking the car when I was sixteen. Consistent with that traumatic event in my life, his somewhat rhetorical questions now seemed eerily similar: "What were you thinking? Who is going to pay for this? Are you drunk?"

I remember leaving the courthouse and running down Main Street to see where my net worth was now harbored. As a twenty-six-year-old, and as a relatively new businessperson, I didn't have $5,000 lying around the house. In fact, I had no idea how I was going to pay for this roughly three-minute "mistake" in my life. As I approached the location, I expected the worst. However, when I arrived at the site, my eyes widened and I looked up to see a building with not one, not two, but five stories! My $5,000 gamble had suddenly procured me a five-story building in the heart of downtown Akron! Move over savvy real estate investors everywhere, there's a new businessman in town!

As the owner of a building on Main Street, I was giddy with excitement and couldn't wait to learn how I could make my hasty purchase into a lucrative opportunity. The building had a rich and successful history. It had been built at the beginning of the twentieth century and was initially a clothing store, then a different clothing store, then later a shoe store until it eventually closed in the 1970s. In early pictures of downtown Akron, you can see that the area had once been a bustling hub of commuters, shoppers, and urban workers that could easily be confused with a street in New York City. But make no mistake, in 1985, downtown Akron was an urban ghost town, and the devolution of the Rust Belt was in full swing.

My enthusiasm would be challenged later that week when I was able to tour the facility. It was warm and sunny as I walked down Main Street during my lunch hour and met my father at the site. It was a good, prideful, and unusual feeling, walking by each building and noticing things I hadn't before. These buildings were now my neighbors. They included weird stone structures of numerous birds, animals, and other creatures I couldn't possibly identify perched in their crevices. My dad was waiting in front of the building, perusing it up and down, looking for something, or anything . . . I didn't know. He had a key that unlocked a padlock, which was connected to a hunk of asymmetrical wood—that was the only way to enter the building. He motioned for me to enter first. I gingerly walked into the building, immediately gathering dust all over my suit with the first few steps. At the time, I only owned three quality suits, and I was mindful of the potential damage that I would have to deal with. There was no electricity in the building, and the only light came from the limited sunlight trying to shine through the dirty, mostly broken windows. My dad had had the foresight to bring a flashlight, and he spread its glow over the first floor. We could see water streaming down the walls and various small puddles spaced around the floor. I gazed up, seeing dozens of plaster pieces and who knows what other kind of material protruding through the ceiling. We continued our path toward the back, taking slow and methodical steps, fully expecting some sort of varmint to mix things up a bit. I was already on edge and knew that I would let out a feminine-sounding yelp should that occur. We made it to the back of the first floor, arriving at the elevator door. For some macho reason, I tried to pry the elevator doors open. Fortunately, I was not successful. Floor by floor we worked our way through the building, finding new and different issues. I could smell many strange and unfamiliar aromas. I didn't know or really want to find out their origin. Let's just say, to quote a Clairol Herbal Essence Shampoo commercial from the 1980s, it was not the smell of "juniper and birch leaves." On the second story, through a small hole in its shabby floor, I could see one of the shimmering puddles on the first floor below us. Every so often we would hear a strange sound, not knowing if it was out on the street somewhere or if something inside had made it. We just looked at each other, not sure what to say, and kept plodding forward. We eventually made it to the top floor, where we saw a rickety ladder attached to the wall, leading to a metal hatch to the roof. It looked like something you would see in a submarine. My dad suggested we climb our way to the top and see what was on the roof. I was thinking I still had time to grab a sandwich before getting back to work and the comfort of my ten key, but as my dad made his way to the ladder, I knew I was out of luck. I followed right behind him as we went up the ladder together. My dad handed me the flashlight as he finagled, jimmied, and eventually pried open the hatch and its crude locking system, letting out several grunts and expletives along the way. We both climbed our way to the top and stood in tight quarters, not far from the entry point, and not knowing which areas were unstable. It occurred to me that no one had been in this spot for probably decades, and perhaps for good reason. We looked in every direction, peering inside the windows of the taller adjacent buildings and doing several 360-degree turns. The sunlight and breeze felt liberating and comforting. We stayed there for a few minutes not saying anything. It took us thirty minutes to get to this spot and less than five minutes to retrace our steps and get back to street level and the reassurance of the known world. What had I gotten myself into? I was a CPA. The bottom line was there was a lot of work ahead for me to get this building into shape, and I didn't quite know what to do next.

Despite my own negative assessment, my dad's perspective gave me some much-needed comfort. After his initial disapproval at the auction, he decided that my blind purchase was a steal, and he started rattling off possibilities for the building's renewed uses. My head was spinning, and I was overwhelmed, unsure how to proceed. Still, my biggest dilemma was how to pay for this building I had naively purchased. Upon reflection, I am sure my dad would have loaned me the money, but at the time, I didn't consider that an option. This was something I had to do myself. As a twenty-six-year-old with decent credit, I was incessantly bombarded with credit card offers. So I did what any semi-irresponsible twenty-six-year-old would do and opened two credit cards, each with $2,500 of available credit, which I used to complete the purchase.

Enter Harvey Nelson. I use the word "enter" loosely here because Harvey had always been in the picture somewhere. Our parents grew up together in tight-knit Akron and were close friends. Even our grandfathers were close, playing cards together every Monday night for more than forty years. Harvey and I had first met in nursery school, and it is jokingly recorded on the company website that he stole my snack on the first day, leaving an indelible mark on both of us. We attended Jewish Sunday school together where mischief was the rule. Our teachers were constantly directing us to the cantor's office to be reprimanded and to have notations put in our "permanent file."

Our bond continued on to Little League baseball, where Harvey's father was the coach and my father was the assistant coach. I mainly played catcher, and Harvey was one of the pitchers. Growing up, I was somewhat of a runt; I usually never made the weight charts. Harvey was on the other end of the spectrum, taller and stronger than most everyone else. We weren't in the same school system, but weekend card games with our clan and events at the Akron Jewish Center kept us connected.

People often contrast us and analyze our relationship. I have always been the more worrisome one, thinking about potential downsides and reluctant to wander into unfamiliar surroundings, while Harvey has always been the free spirit, comfortable in most any setting and eager to try new things and meet new people. If we both got in a cab or an Uber, Harvey would be the one to get in the front seat and strike up a conversation with the driver. By the end of the ride, he would know the driver's blood type. I would be the one in the back, monitoring the cost.

One of my earliest memories of Harvey was of him wearing sneakers to Sunday school. Normally, boys would dress in their suits and ties and girls would wear stately dresses. Everyone had dress shoes. There was surely an unspoken code about it, if not a written rule book. Harvey's sneakers were the talk of all the religious classes that day, and I remember going home in shock to tell my family what had happened. If you analyze this situation, it is probably a classic microcosm of our relationship.

It shouldn't be too surprising that Harvey and I became roommates at the University of Akron, where we lived in an apartment that was both very close to campus and right next to the interstate. You could hear cars humming by twenty-four hours a day. Additionally, our apartment was across the street from a local twenty-four-hour restaurant called Jack Horner's, where we ate almost every one of our meals. While it's not our most commendable business endeavor, Harvey and I were able to afford this "fine dining" because we ran a sports bookmaking operation out of our apartment, in which we took sports bets from fellow students. For two twenty-somethings who understood mathematics and vigorish, running the operation was both comprehensible and quite lucrative. In addition to being able to eat at Jack Horner's every day, our bookmaking operation allowed us to avoid having to work typical college jobs. I think it also gave us some assurance that we could work together in the future.

Ultimately, we had to close the "business" when the possibility of getting caught felt a little too real. During our senior year, Akron's police department made several arrests connected to bookmaking operations throughout the city—all of them more established than our amateurish gambling venture. We were supposed to be relaxing into postgraduation life, but my mind at least was overwhelmed by the hypothetical headline in the local paper: "Two College Students Arrested for Gambling: Careers Ended before They Started." Harvey, with his more carefree approach to life, would have had a more optimistic version: "Two College Students Lauded for Ingenious Business Concept: Unfortunately, Operation Forced to Close." In any event, we both agreed that we needed to move toward a more legitimate vocation. A little sidenote: of all our betting customers, not one person won money overall. That should be a lesson to anyone thinking they can beat the house. Another lesson we learned was that while our personalities and skill sets were different, they were very complementary, enabling us to mesh and become a formidable team.

Naturally, Harvey got involved in my building projects in downtown Akron. We became partners, and together, we brainstormed possible uses for the building. We soon learned that the city of Akron was offering low-interest loans and incentive grants to develop property in downtown Akron. There was only one catch. To be eligible for all of these enticements, you had to include a retail store as part of the property.

So why muffins?

You may be asking yourself—why muffins? It is an often-asked question. At the time, Harvey and I didn't have any solid ideas, and we knew we needed to find a retail concept for the building. Other than cinnamon toothpicks and bookmaking, our experience was limited. So we took a road trip for some inspiration and to visit a friend in Los Angeles. We were aimless, yet curious. During this trip, we visited many cool food establishments: a Thai place that Jack Nicholson allegedly frequented (no, we didn't see him), a trendy drive-in hamburger joint that was all the rage, and many pizza places that all claimed to be the best. One day, we went to what can only be described as a "muffin shop" at an upscale mall. It was the busiest location in the entire mall, and they only sold muffins and coffee. Customers were standing in lines, ten people deep, at 10:00 a.m. on a Tuesday. We couldn't believe it. We were dazzled and intrigued. In that mall, we could see and hear the buzz of attention this shop was getting.

To give this situation some perspective and context, Harvey and I had no food background, no culinary inclination or skill set. I remember in college Harvey once taking a loaf of bread and spreading peanut butter on half of the slices and jelly on the other half as he attempted to eat his way through the loaf. Quite often he did. My culinary taste and expertise weren't that far off from that. At some point during our trip, we had the "aha" moment and started feverishly and compulsively plotting our mission. This wasn't the only inspiration, though. We also figured something popular in California today would eventually be popular in Ohio tomorrow. The portability of a muffin was another factor. There are many handheld foods tied to successful business stories—pizza, cookies, hamburgers, bagels—and muffins were becoming very trendy at the time, showing up more frequently at restaurants and events. So at the end of the trip, we boldly decided that we would put a muffin store on the street-level section of the building and become "Muffin Men."

....

Muffin Recipe #1:
Recognize Opportunities, Awareness of Timing

INGREDIENTS AND DIRECTIONS:
Routinely and continually remind yourself to be aware of timing's importance

Analyze the momentous aspects of situations and try to understand their impact

Consider timing when making significant decisions

Do not take "timing" for granted

BAKING AND PREP TIME:
Hard to tell, but you'll know

THE GAME BEGINS

**It is ok to be in over your head if you
are a very good swimmer.**

—STEVE MARKS

**It's not that I am smart, it's just that
I stay with problems longer.**

—ALBERT EINSTEIN

This undoubtedly will be the first and only time you will see my name near Albert Einstein's, but seeing how I am in control and writing this book, I will take the opportunity to do it.

Once Harvey and I returned from California, we became obsessed with developing the muffin shop. We met every available moment we could to discuss how we would break into the business. We talked about nothing else. I went to sleep at night thinking about it and would wake up eager to start the day. It was a newfound revelation on life.

In January of 1986, I entered the managing partner's office of Coopers and Lybrand and informed him that I was resigning.

"You are going to be opening a muffin shop?" he replied in disbelief. "In downtown Akron?"

The way he said all of this gave me a big pit in my stomach, just like you get right before you're about to accelerate down the hill of a roller coaster. Though I knew the risks of my idea, hearing aloud the doubt in his voice made me nervous. I felt a little chagrinned, wondering if all the excitement over the last six months had clouded my judgment.

Looking back, I don't remember him trying that hard to change my mind. I guess my proclamation may have been too crazy for him to even try to dissuade me. After all, I was giving up on a career with a great company, at which I had been working ever since leaving college, for an uncertain future in the precarious world of retail food sales. I suspected I had damaged my credibility with the firm and would probably be the butt of jokes at the watercooler. It would take more than some embarrassment and a disapproving tone from the managing partner to shake my faith in this venture, though.

I walked out of that mahogany-filled office with a spring in my step, even though I was uncertain how this would all work out. A few weeks later, I packed up my limited belongings and began the trek out the front door. As I passed the "bullpen" where most of my colleagues were located, I heard murmurings of chitchat, mockery, and laughter about my decision and departure. I distinctly heard someone referring to me as the "muffin man," and it wasn't in an endearing fashion. Not everyone at the firm was a skeptic, however. There were several people who were supportive and maybe a bit envious, but I ended up focusing on the detractors and naysayers who were laughing behind my back. It didn't matter because I had a dream and a yearning that was too powerful and consuming to be stopped. It was a life force that I would use to motivate me. Dr. Dietzer was right. Accounting would allow me to go into any business.

I know that I was naive and gullible, not to mention inexperienced. The fact that I was young and carefree, with little to lose, was a strong force that enabled me to leave everything behind and shun the safer and more secure route of being an accountant. I often wonder: if we had we known all that would need to be accomplished, all the possible challenges and difficulties we would encounter, would we have moved forward with our plan? Harvey and I were naive twenty-six-year-old kids. We didn't understand life's downfalls and we lacked the foresight to have any inkling of what we should expect. But we had fortitude, grit, and confidence. Even with that, though, the future was going to be tough.

The tasks ahead of us included:
1. Raising money to start a corporation.
2. Borrowing money to renovate a building.
3. Developing a plan to renovate the building.
4. Renovating the building.
5. Developing a muffin shop concept.
6. Operating a muffin shop.

Complicating these tasks was the following factor:
1. No experience.

Harvey and I started the job of raising money to start our business. We put a business plan together and targeted anybody we knew with money. We first reached out to friends, friends of friends, and parents of friends. The list also included my father and stepmother, who were one of our first investors. I know that they most likely did it out of love, but it still gave us some powerful faith in our abilities.

Harvey and I would meet prospective investors anywhere— coffee shops, bars, kitchens, pool halls, across dining room tables, and at Elks Lodge meetings—and at all hours of the day. We didn't have jobs and were both working from our homes so we could be flexible. We usually made joint presentations, and while we highlighted our business plan, we explained our hopes for the future with passion and vigor.

Dressing in whatever limited professional casual garb we had in our wardrobe, we were prepared: "We want to provide you with an opportunity to invest in something that we are very passionate about and willing to dedicate our lives to for its success," I would start, which cued Harvey to reveal a plate of warm blueberry muffins and push it in the direction of our audience. While we hadn't yet started our development efforts for muffins, we did have some basic blueberry muffin recipes to test.

"We would love to get your impressions on these," Harvey would add.

We were puppy dogs who were eager to please and cunning hawks when tough questions were posed. We could hardly contain our zeal and it became contagious. We liberally name-dropped people we thought would be investing, sometimes exaggerating the situation. Gradually, we refined our pitch, knowing what resonated and what didn't and what jokes to include. Very few people said no.

We knew we needed ample money to not only kick off the business, but also to repair our prized five-story building. Because the building had been built in 1908, it qualified for a tax credit for any new construction, something I knew from my accounting and tax background. This allowed investors to get an immediate return and it was an extra enticement to invest. All in all, we raised about $125,000 from friends and family as well as from an ill-advised small sale of shares to my then girlfriend (the "ill-advised" part of this sentence should probably be in all caps, but the Word document I am writing this book in keeps showing it as an error). We were also able to get an additional $25,000 in matching construction grants for downtown development from the city of Akron.

By virtue of contributing the building to our endeavor, I was able to own a majority share of the company. Harvey, by contributing his efforts in the form of sweat equity, would receive a major stake as well, though it was significantly less than my level. Initially, we both accepted this disparity, but as time went on, it started to create some strife between Harvey and me. I would sometimes play hardball by using my larger percentage ownership to wield power. While that was not my intention, I now understand how I made things difficult for him. This was clearly new territory for me, and I didn't know how to be an effective partner and allow him to feel good about the relationship. These tussles were infrequent enough to not disrupt our workflow, but they continued to simmer. We were so busy that when they would arise, we would simply put them aside as we gathered steam toward building our business.

With our financial momentum rolling, we were able to convince a bank to give us a $150,000 construction loan. The city of Akron had created some additional incentives for people to develop blighted properties downtown, including an interest rate subsidy that allowed our rate to be about 2 percent; pretty good to say the least. Financially speaking, we were ready to go.

Harvey took on the responsibility for the building construction. He requested this assignment, citing his singular experience digging postholes for patio decks one summer. And since my experience was limited to knowing which part of the hammer to hold, he got the job. We started this process in the summer of 1986, and we hoped to open our muffin shop in the summer of 1987. Once again, being naive was a blessing; we had no idea about the difficulties and hurdles we would face. For the most part, we dealt with small contractors who were flexible, creative, and less expensive than the larger outfits.

While Harvey worked full-time at the building, immersing himself in every problem that came up, I was trying to maintain an accounting practice. I would spend whatever time I could at the building, offering my insight. We didn't always agree on solutions and courses of action, and friction would sometimes seep into our conversations. My ego was at work. I wanted to have control, even though Harvey had been working on the problems longer and was an owner too. We had the same goals, however, and so we continued to figure out a way to move things along.

We learned as we went. Harvey became a full-time contractor for our endeavor while I started my own accounting practice to make ends meet. As we continued working simultaneously on our jobs and the company, we started our research and development efforts to learn and understand the art of making muffins. We hired local experts in the field to assist us with making a great product. Instead of paying people to test our product, we brought different types of muffins down to the construction site to get feedback from our construction workers. If they didn't like it, we went back to the "lab" and worked toward getting their approval. We repeated the process endless times, so much so that it became a cornerstone of our recipe development. We didn't follow every last one of the suggestions the workers made; while the tuna fish and celery muffin did make it onto the menu at one point, it was short-lived. We talked endlessly, trying hard to come up with what our concept would look like. We tried to analyze every facet of the operation: What would the display case include? What should be on the menu board? What kind of oven should we buy? Should we grind our own coffee? How much should we charge? Who would do what? The list became endless, the answers changing as frequently as a roulette wheel. Slowly, ever so slowly, though, we could see the concept taking shape.

We met one day to discuss the menu board and what details we should include. It was seemingly an easy project to tackle, but we bickered about what it should look like. I was very vocal about what I envisioned and was not shy in communicating it. I didn't come to the meeting with an open and collaborative mind. That was a mistake, and Harvey and I argued instead of discussing things. We settled on something, but I could sense that our usual demeanors had been altered a bit. I chalked it up to the stressful nature of our situations and was hopeful that things would get better.

The construction efforts proved difficult. We were always moving two steps forward and then finding ourselves three steps behind. We knew very little about the world of construction and what to be prepared for while essentially repurposing a five-story, nearly century-old building. It was certainly a long and arduous learning curve. We had difficulty understanding construction contracts and our ability to change them. There were continual efforts to cut costs while trying to understand the impact of doing so. We tried to get multiple quotes on various elements to get the best prices, though we often weren't making apples-to-apples comparisons. We had to vet subcontractors to make sure they were competent and properly licensed. Vendors had to rely on our ability and knowledge to allocate their efforts at the right time to maximum efficiency. The estimated time for each project always seemed to take longer than expected, causing delays, confusion, and stress.

Fortunately, we were eager to learn, and we weren't easily discouraged about our dream. As time went on, we only grew more obsessed with the building's completion. If we could save any amount of money on something, we were willing to do it ourselves. We did a lot of the small detail work but still got our hands dirty. Hauling, patching, moving, cleaning, prepping, organizing, and errand running were areas where we would pitch in to make the construction run more smoothly. Day after day, we could see the old building's renovation beginning to take shape.

While there was a constant stream of obstacles, our skills and abilities began to sharpen. We started to rely on our experiences, developing an intuition for problem-solving and ultimately gaining confidence in our talents. It was our positive attitude and sense of ownership that kept us going. Out of necessity, we cultivated a tenacious mindset for problem-solving, and we continually pushed ourselves to find creative solutions. We didn't give up at the first, second, or third seemingly impassable roadblocks.

In the spring of 1987, in anticipation of our opening, we started to promote the muffin shop. We visited essentially every business in downtown Akron and told them about our business. We would be selling all-natural, preservative-free muffins in varieties that no one had ever contemplated. Orange Poppyseed, Peanut Butter and Jelly, Raspberry Apple, as well as the traditional Blueberry and Raisin Bran would be available. Often, we would bring warm samples . . . this generally got their attention.

We were able to "rent" a parking space in front of our building. The city allowed you to do this with an application and fee. We scheduled a press conference with the mayor of Akron, Don Plusquellic, a few weeks before our opening. We did interviews with the local TV station as well as with several local radio stations.

My memory of one such radio interview was that it was fabulous and that I dazzled the listening audience, captivating them with every word dripping from my mouth. Unfortunately, an excerpt from a recording I uncovered while writing this book reveals a slightly different scenario.

Radio Announcer: We are here today with Steve Marks, a local entrepreneur, who will be opening a muffin shop in downtown Akron. Steve, you brought in some tasty muffins and we really appreciate that. Tell us what you envision for your muffin shop.

Steve: Ah, well, uh, well, so we will be . . . we hope to be open next week and uh . . . all-natural muffins with uh . . .
Sometimes memories should be left alone.

Despite this quirky performance, I was told by several people that they had heard the broadcast and were excited about our opening. Our visits to downtown businesses, coupled with our radio and tv interviews, were making a difference. We were developing a buzz throughout downtown.

As construction progressed, we picked our opening date: July 17, 1987. However, we needed a surefire way to get people to come to our shop. As a promotion, we decided to offer "free muffins" to every customer. Our hope was that they wouldn't just take the free muffin, but would instead be grateful enough for the free one that they'd buy more. We redoubled our efforts with downtown businesses and communicated this freebie offer. The final piece of the puzzle was to arrange for a band to perform on the rented parking space. We were all set for a grand opening never seen before in Akron.

On June 25, 1987, about three weeks before our grand opening, I went to the work site one morning to check on things. Shortly after my arrival, Harvey came up to me with a concerned look on his face and handed me a sealed envelope.

"Read this and we can talk," he said.

I opened the envelope and revealed a six-page letter from Harvey:

Dear Sme: ("Sme" was my childhood nickname.)

I am sure you are wondering what this letter is all about. I have a feeling before I write any further that this is something I should have written long ago.

I feel we have a definite problem with our working relationship. I think we are two different kinds of people, whom as friends, can accept our differences and rise above them to create and sustain a great "friendship" relationship. This is obvious since we've been through so much together as pals or whatever you want to call it and have stayed together for so long . . .

The letter went on to indicate his dissatisfaction with our working relationship, citing numerous (and valid) situations. He was addressing how we needed to make substantive changes if we were going to continue on as business partners. He said he wanted to have a meeting where we would document our responsibilities, how we should interact with other employees, how we would work together, and methods by which to operate.

The letter was a gut punch. I read and reread it several times and wasn't sure how to react. Harvey was obviously hurting, and I had been oblivious (or so I told myself) to his discomfort and uneasiness. We were both under a lot of pressure with our perceived futures on the line. I stewed over the letter all day, rotating between being upset, being defensive, or trying to combat his assessment of our state of affairs. We agreed to have a preliminary meeting at the end of the day to decide what to do. As we interacted throughout the day on the job site, there was a certain uncomfortableness that had never really existed between the two of us before—we'd been friends for nearly all of our lives. It was an ugly feeling, and it heightened my concern about how this would all get resolved.

As the day reached an end, the tension seemed to mount. I was nervous about a lot of things: for starters, our friendship, the business, and the future. We had enough challenges fighting those forces that weren't in our camp. We agreed to meet in a quiet area of the building. There were no chairs in the room, so we just sat down on the floor and used the unfinished wall as support. Harvey began by going over the letter in a little more detail, but it didn't take long before I understood his position. We went back and forth, each of us getting to the point where our voices were cracking with emotion. We were near the breaking point anyway, and though this meeting wasn't helpful to our well-being, it needed to be done. We talked for hours, taking a brief break for some pizza. We continued afterward, eventually agreeing that we needed to put together some sort of document we could potentially refer to so that we would both be on the same page. We set up a meeting in two days to put this manifesto together. Although anxiety would fester for a few more days after that, we were both a little relieved that we had cleared the air. Hopefully we would be better for it.

On June 27, we had an early morning meeting to begin the process. We met for several hours, pounding out an eleven-page, handwritten document that included four articles, an appendix, and a signature page. It dealt with every conceivable issue that we thought we might face. It dealt with communication, attitudes, dealing with people, dealing with girlfriends, functional guidelines, employee relations, legal matters, and rules of engagement. It culminated with a detailed list of responsibilities. Our founding fathers would have been proud. Hell, we were proud. We were on the same page, and we left the building that day as better friends, each of us with a deeper appreciation for what it takes to keep one another together.

As we look back on that document today, it's eerie how many things we've followed throughout our thirty-plus-year partnership. I don't remember looking at the document too many times, so it would appear we each had it stored in our internal operating system. I am fortunate that Harvey had the fortitude to initiate this crossroad decision point and put us on the right path for the future. If we could get through this, we were confident we could get through just about anything.

We realized as we approached the opening date, July 17, the timeline for completing the building would be very tight. As I'm sure most people in the business can relate to, construction never goes the way you expect it to. The mere nature of a construction timeline, coupled with our lack of experience dealing with contractors, only exacerbated the issue. It was coming down to the wire. We had many discussions with the building department, and controversial issues were the norm. Our interpretations were usually wrong. The daily battles were zapping our strength and lengthening the time it took to complete various functions. We wanted to order inventory, but we didn't have the space complete to store anything. Our signage wasn't installed. The electricity needed to be finished so we could operate equipment, use the phone system, and operate the cash register. We didn't even have locks on the doors yet.

We couldn't possibly change the date of the grand opening since we had blasted our intention throughout the city. We had been on radio stations, we'd held a press conference, and we had spread the word to anyone who would listen to us about it. We were going to open no matter what, and the building department knew we had to be absolutely finished with the building before we opened.

Every day was packed with pressure, and we used a lot of energy trying to determine if we could make it. The day before our grand opening, it became apparent that we would not be finished. We were at a standstill. Everyone knew what the stakes were, and no one was going to blink. We were emotionally invested in every little aspect of the construction, and we were constantly arguing with the building department about siding in our direction. We went back and forth. Arguments, disagreements, and veiled legal threats were the order of the day. I am not sure who wore down who first, but as the opening date got closer, tension and stress were mounting on both sides. We asked for a meeting with the building department to try and figure out a way, any way, to open the business.

On the day of the meeting, I woke up with a very uneasy feeling, not knowing what would transpire. At the time, I felt it was the most important day of my life and could easily move in many different directions. A lot of people were relying on us, and not opening as planned would be a major defeat. Harvey and I both walked into the meeting, looking more beaten than confident. We stated our case. We mostly complained, but we also tried to convey the importance of opening on time. The building department had rules. We kept poking at ways around them, looking for loopholes. I am sure we looked desperate, and I think they could sense we weren't going away without a satisfactory resolution. After a lot of back and forth, we came up with a plan and a compromise. If we would make some immediate, minor, temporary modifications to the site, the building department would grant us a provisional occupancy permit. We all agreed. With just sixteen hours to go before our grand opening, we'd averted our first potential catastrophe. We would make our grand opening.

....

Muffin Recipe #2:
A Need to Embrace Problem-Solving

INGREDIENTS AND DIRECTIONS:

Embrace problem-solving as a necessary and vital part of business

Develop problem-solving systems and attributes as part of your infrastructure

Surround yourself with people who excel at problem-solving (and reward problem-solvers)

Understand that problems flow to the successful

BAKING AND PREP TIME:

Especially in the early stages

THE GRAND OPENING

**If you own your own business,
you are never late to work.**

—STEVE MARKS

On a warm, sunny Friday, July 17, 1987, we opened our doors at 7:00 a.m. People were lined up around the block! We had friends and family in the kitchen, cranking out muffins as fast as possible. It was a madhouse! It was like a wedding, bar mitzvah, and graduation party all wrapped up together. We had so many people we knew who were coming to show support as well, like downtown employees, politicians, vendors, and our construction workers. The crowds were robust all day, and we never took a breather until we closed at 5:00 p.m. We were stunned. We were even more stunned when we learned that more than 2,000 customers had come through our doors that first day. Yes, some of them only wanted the free muffins, but most others bought something significant. We were in business, but we didn't know what in the hell to do next.

While the opening day was fantastic, reality stepped in the following Monday as we officially opened for business and grappled with all the necessary duties and functions of operating a retail store. We had taken a small breather after the grand opening, but Monday came too quickly for us and we were thrown back into the fire. Over the next several weeks, we had numerous issues come up that weren't necessarily on our radar. We continually juggled the menu, adding and subtracting items based upon customer feedback. Certain employees didn't work out. Our equipment malfunctioned.

Recipes didn't turn out the way we expected them to.

We learned as we went, relying on vendors and advisors. We worked hard at building a loyal following. We added soups, salads, sandwiches, cookies, and brownies. We made plenty of mistakes and misjudgments, which caused us to think more about our failures and disappointments. Through it all, however, we never quit moving forward.

Our muffin shop was very close to the University of Akron, so logically, it was in our best interest to find a way to tap into the population of the roughly twenty-five thousand students there. Using one of the carpenters who had helped with the construction of the building, we built a portable muffin shop to close the small gap of distance between us and the university. Though we intended it to resemble our established storefront, the cart that could hold several dozen muffins ultimately ended up looking more like a twelve-year-old's Soap Box Derby car. Even so, whenever sales weren't on track for a good day on Main Street, we would take the cart up to the university.

We weren't allowed to sell on campus, so we would push the cart right along the boundary. It was very popular with the students, and to this day, many people remind me that they first tried our muffins through this channel. Unfortunately, the cart was extremely heavy, and our path to the university traversed two large hills. Harvey was the only one who could push the cart up the hill and consequently, we had to work around his schedule to make sales. This particular hurdle, no pun intended, wasn't something they specifically taught us in business school. Maybe they should have.

Six months after we opened, we received a curious phone call. A man who owned a diner wanted to know if he could buy our muffins in batter form, take it back to his restaurant, and then bake and serve them to his customers. Interesting. We were somewhat skeptical and shortsighted about this. Would this situation affect sales? How would this impact our operations? After some discussion, we reasoned that it was worth the risk to explore the wholesale world, and we reluctantly decided to sell our muffin batter to this customer—with some conditions. We felt we needed to have the upper hand, and we made things somewhat difficult for our first prospective wholesale customer. They had to come at 5:00 p.m. when we closed, they had to bring a check, and they had to bring their own buckets! Amazingly, the diner owner jumped through all these hoops and we had our first wholesale customer.

A few days passed and he came back, wanting to replenish his supply. A few more days went by and he came back again, wanting to expand into other varieties. This went on for some time before we realized that this was an opportunity we needed to jump on. We immediately went to work. We created price lists. We found a bucket manufacturer ourselves, eliminating the need for our customers to bring back buckets themselves (you can imagine the food safety issues this avoided). We refined our production system. We started to ponder the possibilities. Who else could we sell to? How would we handle the increased workload? Who would do what? We were excited about this new direction and talked incessantly about the possibilities.

At the time, the only real way for a retailer to sell a quality muffin product was to buy all the necessary ingredients, mix them, store them, and bake the muffins. This was a labor-intensive and inefficient process for a retailer, and so our concept became a clear competitive advantage. The landscape was wide open for us to expand the business.

This time in our lives was very exciting. We woke up every day with optimism and eagerness to move things along. After work, when we went home, we thought about nothing else but the business. It was clearly our passion and we were having the time of our lives. This is why entrepreneurs become entrepreneurs. The business was our obsession, and we never looked at anything we were doing as work.

After obtaining that first wholesale customer and working through all the difficulties and impediments, we started to ponder additional accounts. After all, we now had a success story we could communicate to new prospects. We targeted three or five other local businesses and started making calls to get appointments. Most of the prospects we called made it relatively easy to get an appointment and make a presentation. We came armed with fresh-baked muffins, a couple of buckets of muffin batter to leave behind, and a simple price list. Put a warm, fresh-baked muffin in front of someone and amazing things can happen.

I don't remember hearing the word "pivoting" in college or when we first started out, but now it is a relatively common term in business. It generally involves a dramatic shift in strategy. We were somewhat anxious going through this process of exploring the wholesale side of the business. We had made certain assumptions and had clear-cut goals about what we envisioned for the business. Now they were all in question. One of the biggest dilemmas facing an entrepreneur is deciding on the right method and timing for a potential pivot. This quandary was staring us in the face. We had to seriously evaluate our options, look at the pros and cons, and make a decisive commitment. Fortunately, we had created an environment where we could discuss, strategize, and eventually implement our plan.

I think the fact that Harvey and I both had such intimate familiarity with every aspect of the business was an effective tool to evaluate our potential pivot into wholesale. Our initial business plan actually called for the company to add retail outlets and possibly a franchise component. Moving our focus to wholesale would be a major turning point. As you will read later in our story, our second pivot happened when we started to face stiff competition from a national company that had better distribution, a powerful sales team, and the wherewithal to go after business with a cutthroat mentality. To compete with this national business, we decided to develop a customer approach that would be difficult to compete against. Our relatively small size and our ability to be nimble and adaptive became an advantage.

The question I get asked most of the time is, "What is your favorite muffin?" My favorite muffin is the muffin with the highest gross profit margin.
—STEVE MARKS

Our call to a local gourmet market went very well, and they agreed to try the product we left behind and get back to us. A few days later, we followed up with them and learned that they loved the product and wanted to put it into their bakery case as soon as possible. While they made muffins from scratch, it was labor-intensive. It was also difficult to procure all the ingredients necessary to make an ample variety of products.

We provided them with a great solution, which allowed for a good gross margin. One problem we encountered was that the wholesale buyers wanted the products delivered. We didn't have the luxury of asking all our customers to pick up the product. Their delivery requirement created a whole new series of problems for us. The product needed to remain cold (thirty-two to forty degrees). We didn't have a delivery vehicle that could keep product at that temperature. Our solution was to use our own cars, using thermal blankets to cover the batter. Fortunately, the gourmet market was only fifteen minutes away and we could get away with this. It wasn't the most distinguished delivery plan, but we had a distribution system.

Gradually, we built our wholesale muffin batter business. We caught the attention of a local distributor who kept seeing our buckets around town. In the wholesale food business, distributors are somewhat vital for growth as they can help you reach a much larger clientele. They store your product along with many others, and they use a fleet of temperature-controlled vehicles to sell to a particular geographical region. We needed a distributor because our business was growing, which made it difficult for us to keep up ourselves. Also, a distributor would open our business up to many more prospects.

There were issues, however. Because our product was all-natural and preservative-free and we weren't freezing it, the product only had a shelf life of about five days. This wasn't very practical for a distributor who needed to stock product for their customers weeks in advance. We experimented with frozen product, and with some small modifications, we made it work while maintaining the product's all-natural and preservative-free aspects. A customer would have to merely buy frozen muffin batter and store it in their freezer, and then when they needed product, they could thaw it in the cooler overnight. Thaw, scoop out, and bake. Switching to frozen product opened up many opportunities for efficiency. We could keep stock product and be ahead of demand. We were also fortunate that distributors were beginning to embrace frozen products. In 1988, we added our first distributor and moved toward a significant pivot for the company.

....

Muffin Recipe #3:
An Ability to Master the Art of the Pivot

INGREDIENTS AND DIRECTIONS:

Promote an environment for recognizing potential pivots

Don't fall in love with a strategy as your sole driving force

Challenge assumptions that you have created

When you do pivot, do it as quickly as possible and realign your goals

BAKING AND PREP TIME:

At key moments

OUR FIRST EXPANSION AND THE GOLDEN ARCHES

Nothing in the world can take the place of persistence. Talent will not: nothing is more common than unsuccessful men with talent. Genius will not; unrewarded genius is almost a proverb. Education will not; the world is full of educated derelicts. Persistence and determination alone are omnipotent.

—CALVIN COOLIDGE

Construct your determination with Sustained Effort, Controlled Attention, and Concentrated Energy. Opportunities never come to those who wait . . . they are captured by those who dare to attack.

—PAUL J. MEYER

The above quotes really resonate with me, especially as an entrepreneur. As I think back on my career, I've realized that the concepts of persistence, determination, and a sense of urgency are common threads throughout. For example, I was struck by how many of our largest sales accomplishments were the result of this persistence mentality. How many times did we contemplate giving up on a certain potential account only to be eventually rewarded with a loyal and profitable customer?

A sense of urgency is the lifeblood of any entrepreneur. This attribute is primarily a benefit, but it can sometimes be a curse.

It's the mentality of continuously focusing on your goals, your strategy, and the tasks required to achieve them. It's also about internally developing appropriate deadlines. It is being aware of what is important, of what needs to be done now and what can wait. It is a constant calculus facing the entrepreneur that can portend success or disappointment. Personally, I am cursed with an inclination to want everything accomplished "now," and I have continuously had to struggle with balancing this with the real world, where delays and obstacles are inevitable.

This concept is a valuable building block for any business. It is why marathon runners struggle for 26.2 miles, pushing themselves to the limit to finish a race. It is why explorers spend their whole lives without success and then achieve a breakthrough by discovering a new land. It is why, after countless failures, a revolutionary invention is created. Thomas Edison often spoke of his continued failures in developing the light bulb: "I have not failed. I've just found 10,000 ways that won't work." We need to appreciate that most of our designs and desires won't work as planned. In business, it's often (if you're lucky) three steps forward and two steps back. Those that have the moxie to withstand the disappointments and setbacks that are inevitable in business are the ones who will prove to be successful.

Growing pains were coming by the hour. We were running out of all kinds of space—storage space, freezer space, and workspace. We were working out of a small kitchen that was being used not only to prepare product for the muffin shop's daily activity, but also to produce muffin batter for our wholesale business. We decided to expand our production space by renovating our building's basement. As part of the original renovation, the second floor was fitted for office space, and I conveniently moved my accounting practice there. The third and fourth floors remained idle, but they were ready for renovation if an opportunity arose. The basement production space would require going back to the bank for the needed funds. This was not going to be an easy sell. At the time, we were at best marginally profitable, although the sales side of our business was growing rapidly. And without the new space, we couldn't grow any further.

We went back to our bank with a logical request for funds to renovate the basement as well as to buy a much-needed walk-in freezer to store product for future sales. We also needed a professional mixer instead of the large bowl we were using to mix ten pounds of product at a time. We needed $100,000. After hearing our presentation and rationale, the bank eventually agreed to our request, but only if we could get someone, in addition to Harvey and me, to guarantee the loan—essentially someone with real credit. Without much hesitation, my father and stepmother agreed to be our guarantors. I was very fortunate and grateful that they did this, but I was not sure if they did this for business reasons or simply because I was their son. I know that they believed in me and that's all that really mattered. In any event, we had our funds.

After six months of renovation, the basement was complete, and we began to pursue more wholesale accounts. We looked at the makeup of our distributors' customers. The most prevalent type of accounts they serviced were frozen yogurt shops. Why frozen yogurt shops, you ask? Frozen yogurt shops serve most of their product after the noon hour, so the morning hours had become an opportunity to sell breakfast products, including coffee, pastries, and drumroll . . . muffins! This became a very good match for us; these yogurt shops were struggling to differentiate themselves, and fresh-baked muffins were an excellent addition.

We enthusiastically went after this retail segment, meeting with yogurt shop owners throughout northeastern Ohio. Once again, it was a relatively easy sales presentation. The barriers for them to start selling fresh-baked muffins proved very small. All these stores needed were some minor renovations and an oven. Yogurt shops became a successful niche business, and we continued to grow one store at a time. We eventually added cookie dough and brownies to our lineup, which catered to the yogurt shops' more significant daytime business.

While we were building the wholesale business, the retail business chugged along, but something didn't seem quite right. We were spending equal amounts of time on both the retail and wholesale sectors, but the wholesale business was expanding much more rapidly. While the retail business had a very loyal following, it wasn't growing at nearly the same rate as our wholesale side. Additionally, the problems with retail were much more abundant and bothersome. Theft, isolated customer complaints, and operational problems were all factors that affected our retail operation, though they were less significant with our wholesale business.

During this phase of our business, we received a call from a local McDonald's. Yes, that McDonald's—golden arches, Big Macs . . . you know the one. After a chance visit to our shop, local franchise owners John Blickle and Richard Heidman had one of their staff members call us to ask if we were interested in testing a fresh-baked muffin program in their restaurants. I initially thought it was a practical joke, something my friends would do without hesitation. Fortunately, I detected this call as genuine. After I hung up the phone, I jumped up from my seat and screamed, "We are going to be selling to McDonald's!"

In every conversation Harvey and I had with anyone who would listen over the following weeks, we managed to include a passing reference to doing business with McDonald's. It was very exciting, and we could only imagine the possibilities.

McDonald's asked if they could do a test with six stores. They would buy our batter in buckets, scoop them into pans, and bake muffins in their biscuit ovens. In the summer of 1989, we started selling them fresh-baked muffins. Sales were fantastic. The likely reason: we paid everyone we knew to buy out every muffin McDonald's made. We weren't necessarily proud of this tactic, but our friends really liked the idea of getting free muffins.

After a few weeks, McDonald's expanded the test to fifteen stores throughout Summit County. We responded by getting more friends to buy product. After a few more weeks, McDonald's decided to put the muffins in all their local stores, roughly thirty locations. We were running out of friends as well as the money to reimburse them for their purchases. Grudgingly, we determined we would let true market forces determine our fate. After a few more weeks, sales were still going strong, even without our undercover customers. McDonald's was very happy, and we envisioned muffins in every restaurant in America. They started advertising our muffins on their marquees and sales continued to climb. I remember driving by a McDonald's and craning my neck to see the sign for as long as possible. That will always be an indelible feeling.

By this time, I had broken up with the girlfriend I mentioned previously. I should probably revise that sentence. By this time, I was over the heartache of being dumped by my former girlfriend and fellow shareholder. It was a devastating and emotional experience for me, something I had never encountered before. I had a hard time coming to grips with this rejection. It was something I couldn't understand. Upon reflection, I realize I had used this rejection to fuel my determination to accomplish many of my goals and foster my work ethic. In a strange way, I wanted to prove that her decision to dump me was wrong.

This was like leaving the offices of Coopers and Lybrand and hearing the murmurs of laughter for starting a muffin shop. Both circumstances were motivating and inspiring forces for me. This chip on my shoulder turned out to be an important life force that I utilized to overcome struggles and challenges. Right around this time, my good friend and cousin, Bob Littman, called me to line up a blind date for me. I would just need to call her and set it up. I trusted Bob and was confident in his judgment.

However, I had set policies and concepts for dating . . . a dating code of regulations, if you will. The distance to the date's house had to be under twenty minutes. First dates were lunches, and if they were successful, they would be followed up by weeknight dates. Eventually, if there was chemistry, I would take the daring step of organizing a date for a weekend night date. I think you get the picture. As suggested, I called Jeannine Barry to set up our first lunch.

It took just under nineteen minutes to get her apartment; close, but under the requirement. I remember going up the steps to her apartment, not sure what to expect. She had already agreed to a weekday lunch so that was a good sign. The door opened to a smiling, beautiful woman, who, in the words of Renée Zellweger in *Jerry McGuire*, "had me at hello." We did the small talk dance, and I didn't say anything stupid. So far, so good. Off we went.

I had picked her up in my used 1985 Audi. It had been recalled for a variety of reasons, and I was having continual problems with it. One of these problems involved having to keep the rear backdoor window ajar in order to get the air conditioning to work. Another one involved pressing the flashers once before the radio would come on. It was a comedy of errors as we made our way to a downtown Akron lunch spot. Jeannine could only laugh at my car snafus, which put me at ease. If it all went well, we would visit the muffin shop for me to captivate her in my lair, impressing her with my new, expanding business.

We sat down at a nice table. During this period, I was constantly on some weird eating kick. For some time, I would only eat Grape Nuts for breakfast. Another time, I only ate fruit and nuts before noon. I have always been into health, and I've always tried to eat right, but I often took it to an extreme. I was always searching for the ultimate food regimen. I gave up red meat and pork just after college and haven't had it since. But this didn't seem to sway Jeannine at all. As I listened to her order a cheeseburger, fries, and a milkshake, I was thinking about how she might interpret my menu selection. I selected the halibut, cooked only in lemon water, no butter, with steamed veggies and only vinegar for my salad. I could hear her eyes rolling in her head.

After lunch, we went back to the muffin shop for a tour. I alerted everyone there that I might be coming back and to make sure they looked and spoke to me with reverence. Except for Harvey, most everybody followed directions. Everything was going as planned. I eventually took Jeannine back to her apartment and walked her up the steps. I knew I wanted another date, but did she feel the same way? We got to the top of the steps. There was very little room to stand if the door wasn't open, and our faces were very close to one another. I gambled and moved in for a kiss. In case you're wondering, this was not in my dating code. We kissed softly, and I asked her if she would like to go out again. She said yes.

After a few weeks, we were together all the time, and she became part of the roller-coaster ride of our business and the rest of my life. I was now exposed to the dilemma of balancing home and work life.

Jeannine was a great supporter, and there weren't too many situations where I had to choose, but there was a new dynamic and it took some time and effort to get used to. There were now two very important pillars in my life that would become a factor in every decision that would be made. Eventually, another important pillar and complexity, in the form of kids, would happen. My mindset also went through a logical transformation . . . it was now a team sport.

Meanwhile, our delivery van was running ragged, trying to transport muffins to all thirty McDonald's locations on a regular basis, but we couldn't help but try to keep growing the business. John Blickle, from McDonald's, who had first called us to inquire about a test, was not only the co-owner and president of the local McDonald's franchise, but he was also a prominent member of the regional franchise group, a collection of other franchisees with stores throughout northeastern Ohio. He offered to talk to this co-op, a total of about 150 locations, on our behalf. But the real gem was that he would talk to their distributor about delivering the products to all these restaurants, including his local stores.

We were overwhelmed with such a perfect offer laid out in front of us and very grateful to John for wanting to do this. We were fully committed to getting into the McDonald's distribution system and expanding our business. However, there was one small catch. We had to convince a majority of the franchisees to take on our product in their restaurants. It would come down to a vote from each franchise owner and a majority vote would rule. A lot was riding on their decision. Would we be able to expand our operation, or would we have to be satisfied with what we had?

In 1991, our strategy with the McDonald's franchisees was to meet with as many of them as possible before the co-op meeting. We could explain our program and hopefully get their support for the all-important vote taking place in a few weeks. We particularly focused on the more influential and vocal franchisees as it was likely the co-op meeting would be a lively debate. We needed a consensus from the franchisees in favor of our product. After every individual presentation, we would ask for their support and a favorable vote at the co-op meeting. If the answer was no, we worked feverishly to overcome their objections. Our sales presentation emphasized our current sales numbers (about thirty muffins per day, per store) and the gross margin they would make (about 50 percent). And we always arrived with some warm muffins at meetings that were targeted between 9:00 and 10:00 a.m.

In our view, the sales of muffins in their stores would be incremental, meaning they wouldn't take away sales from the other, more stable products and they would be a welcome addition to the menu. We were determined to meet with as many McDonald's franchisees as possible. When a member of our sales team asked me how long they should call on a particular McDonald's before giving up, my response came pretty quickly.

"That depends."

"Depends on what?" they'd respond.

"It depends on which one of you dies first."

My persistent and determined mindset became something I took a lot of pride in, and I believe it was an important aspect of our success. We ultimately made presentations to almost every McDonald's franchisee in the region.

The day finally came for our McDonald's co-op presentation and the vote on installing Main Street Muffins in all the McDonald's locations in northeastern Ohio. We had prepared for the day with a clear understanding with what was at stake. The meeting included about fifteen individual owners, twenty of their staff, ten or so people from the McDonald's corporate office, and the distributor who would be responsible for getting the product to each location. We met at a Cleveland hotel. Harvey and I brought all kinds of props, including fresh-baked muffins. We made our presentation to the group, repeating many of the same things we had said in our one-on-one meetings. We anticipated many of the issues we knew would come up based on our experience at the previous meetings. When the presentation was done, a barrage of questions came at us. We answered all of them carefully and methodically. Fortunately, our field visits to the franchisees proved valuable. We knew what to expect and responded with proper answers that we knew would mollify them based upon that groundwork.

After the discussion ended, they called for a vote and began to call the name of each franchisee. Surprisingly, they allowed us to stay in the meeting. We quickly realized that we would be able to see each owner as they put forth their vote. Our intensity heightened. We would soon know our fate. I made sure that I could establish eye contact with each and every owner as they put forth their vote. I reasoned that if they had supported me in the earlier meeting, they wouldn't back down now, especially with me staring them down, looking like an eager puppy that hadn't eaten for a while. One by one the votes came in, and I didn't blink once they started. When the final tally was done, we got more than the necessary votes . . . it was almost unanimous! We now had 150 new customers! We had no idea how we were going to handle this amount of product and distribution, but we didn't care. It was a great milestone for the company, and for now, we were going to enjoy the moment. We were officially selling to the largest restaurant chain in the world!

We were at another crossroads. How could we possibly expand our production so quickly? We were determined to come up with a viable new approach for production. It was Harvey who ultimately came up with using the concept of "team piece work"; that is, paying an employee by what they produce, rather than by the hour. This production concept became the answer to many of our growing pains. Once we were able to determine the exact labor cost of producing a pound of product, we implemented a plan to pay our production team for the number of pounds they produced. By now, we had a production crew of about nine people. If they were able to produce at a faster pace than the standard, they would make more money and we would have a lower cost per pound (as well as increased capacity).

We learned a very valuable lesson: never underestimate the power of incentives! Our production capacity tripled overnight with this new system! Our employees doubled, and in some cases, tripled their pay due to their increased production. They worked in three-person teams. They worked as a team and were compensated as a team. They pressured each other to work faster and more efficiently. We were pleasantly surprised and astounded by their work. This experience would prove valuable, and it helped us learn how to treat future employees. It was important to us that our employees wanted to come to work motivated to do a good job. I believe this attitude is a major reason why we have had so many great employees over the years. In this initial case, the new system allowed us to meet the increased demand and move on to other, more complex issues. We were happy with the outcome, and the production team was happy with their higher paychecks. This situation also created loyalty among our employees, an outcome we would also work hard to cultivate in the future.

As we were gearing up for the growth of our wholesale business, we made another bold decision. While we had pivoted initially to the wholesale element, it was not yet the fundamental core of the business. This would be a crucial moment in our company history as we shifted our focus, drive, and attention to our wholesale element and divested from the retail business. This required a major switch in philosophy, as well as some major logistical efforts. Our identity was the retail store on Main Street. How would it look if we just closed our doors? Could we give up the retail sales and still be financially viable? Many questions had to be addressed. We ultimately had the idea to "give" our retail operation away under a license arrangement where the licensees would agree to buy our muffin batters and cookie dough. We included some other requirements as well, like quality control and the limited use of the company name. It was an idea that solved several issues at once. We could maintain a good chunk of the sales by selling our batters and doughs via the wholesale route, and our retail store would remain viable and continue to have a presence.

We found a local restaurant owner who owned another operation a few doors down the street. He was excited to take over our retail store and pay us rent for use of the space. This was not an easy decision for us, seeing as we had our blood, sweat, and tears wrapped up in this muffin shop and we were about to leave it in the hands of someone else. However, we ultimately knew it was the right strategic move and it had to be made. There would be no turning back. We were well on our way to becoming an exclusively wholesale business. But we would still need a place to produce more of our product if we wanted to truly expand.

We started our search by asking realtors and government officials for leads and ideas. It was important for us to stay in Akron, so that became one of the requirements for our new space. It needed to have space for offices, production, a loading dock, and ideally, a large freezer, which would narrow down our possible choices. We also couldn't take on a building that would require more renovation and money, so that became a factor as well.

The search took several weeks and culminated when the city of Akron told us about a possible location. A few short miles away from our downtown location stood a building owned by Summit Fish, a wholesale distributor of fish products. They were selling their building. It was built in the 1950s and had a freezer that could hold more than 100,000 pounds of product. It was a big jump from our freezer in the basement on Main Street that was ten feet by ten feet. This new building was 15,000 square feet, and it included production space, office space, three docks, and storage space. We negotiated a lease with an option to buy. A few short months later, we turned over the keys to our retail store and moved into our plant in the appropriately named Opportunity Park, an industrial neighborhood just south of downtown Akron.

Summit Fish moved everything out of the building except the fish smell. It took a lot of lemons, disinfectant, and chlorine to get to the point where our clothes didn't smell like dead fish after a long day at the office. Ironically, there is more on fish later in this story.

In 1992, Senator John Glenn was gearing up for a reelection campaign in Ohio. During this time, we were also planning our grand opening at the new production facility. Someone in our office had a relative in Glenn's office, and they arranged for him to visit during our facility's grand opening celebration. We were lucky enough to get him to come.

October 11, 1992, our grand opening, was a great day as Harvey introduced Senator Glenn and his wife, Annie, to dozens of supporters, area politicians, media, and our roughly fifteen employees. The senator spoke for twenty minutes and talked glowingly about our products and operation. We were elated. I remember seeing the proud expression on my dad's face, which made the day extra special. After the senator's speech, he stayed and mingled for more than an hour, shaking hands and sampling more of our product offerings. I had a picture taken of my then six-month-old son, Wyatt, and the senator; it still sits in my home office today. After his visit, we famously came up with the following claim that would be embedded in our history and eventually memorialized on the company website:

1992: Astronaut John Glenn visits Main Street Muffins. He officially becomes the only person to have orbited the earth and eaten a Blueberry Main Street Muffin. His comment: "They are out of this world." *(illustration by Brady Marks)*

One of the periodicals we read during this time was *Inc.* magazine, and we gained a lot of insight into the travails and successes of other entrepreneurs. Every year, the magazine created a list called the "Inc. 500," a collection of the fastest-growing companies in the US. At the end of 1992, we submitted our sales data in the hopes of making this prestigious list. One day, we received a letter from *Inc.* informing us that we had the made the list and that our name would be included in their annual publication. Main Street Muffins was now one of the fastest growing companies in the US. Some nice affirmation. I remember Harvey saying that it was "cool," but that it would be better to be included in *Forbes*'s list of the world's wealthiest individuals. One step at a time . . .

Over the next few years, we also started to win some local awards for our sales growth. In 1993, we submitted an application to the US Small Business Administration for the Small Business Persons of the Year Award. We were stunned a few months later to find out we had won and that part of our award included a visit with President Bill Clinton, who was coming to Akron for a campaign visit at the city's Civic Theatre, just a few doors down from our building on Main Street. On the day of his visit, Harvey and I arrived at the venue and were eventually ushered to a back room at the theatre with about a dozen dignitaries from the region. We clearly seemed out of place. There were politicians, clergy, big donors, and . . . two muffin men holding a small box of pastries.

It was surreal as we watched the president enter the room to raucous applause and saw him being introduced to several people before us. I was captivated with how he looked at and engaged with each and every person, never straying his eyes around the room. Forget about your political affiliation or opinion, it's hard to describe the aura and charisma that he effused. But he had it and he knew how to use it. My interaction with the president was memorable, not because of the depth and meaningfulness of our conversation, but more for the embarrassing sounds my mouth emitted in my attempt to be clever, entertaining, and interesting. I handed him a box of our muffins and said something about muffins on Air Force One and blah, blah, blah. If there were more people in the room, it would have easily made my top ten list of my most embarrassing moments. But I learned a valuable lesson from meeting President Clinton: don't try to match magnetism and witty banter with someone who does it effortlessly and extraordinarily well.

That year, as the recipient of one of those local awards, I was invited to a small dinner party for former US Secretary of State Henry Kissinger. I was to be seated next to him at the dinner table. I was determined to be prepared for the engagement and I read his biography, written by famed author Walter Isaacson. It was more than 900 pages and took me more than three months to get through it! When the moment came, I told Kissinger that I had read his biography and had some questions for him. He asked me, "Which one?" I was taken aback. Which question? No, he wanted to know which biography I had read. I told him I'd read the one written by Isaacson. There was a pause as he got visibly upset, telling me the book was "terrible" and that "Isaacson didn't do a very good job." I had no idea that there were multiple biographies and that I had read the worst of them. My questions became inane. It still was a great dinner, hearing his stories and such, but the lesson learned was that even the best intentions and preparation may not be successful.

These interactions afforded me a bird's-eye view of how these amazingly accomplished individuals interact and how revered they can be. I learned very quickly to try to stay in the moment and that I should also try to see the potential importance of each interaction. It's not likely that these lessons will be found in any business book, but these encounters had important and positive life-changing effects on me. Each occasion left me with a very valuable, though maybe a little embarrassing, lesson.

In 1992, we got call from Akron General, one of our local hospitals. They wanted to do a fundraiser, selling our muffins to area residents. The intention was to raise money for women who couldn't afford breast cancer screening services. We had always strived to be a good corporate citizen, but our efforts were somewhat limited to donating muffins and other bakery products that were left over at the end of the day to local charitable organizations. However, this event would elevate our commitment to and involvement in the community.

We met with the hospital's staff and put together a concept called "Muffins for Mammograms," using our product and both of our workforces to sell it. We had a lot of fun designing the T-shirt (you can use your imagination). And in October 1992, during National Breast Cancer Awareness Month, Muffins for Mammograms was launched. It was a huge success, raising thousands of dollars. The event would continue throughout our history, winning awards for creativity, ultimately raising hundreds of thousands of dollars, and genuinely saving lives.

···

Muffin Recipe #4:
A Persistent and Determined Mindset and a Sense of Urgency

INGREDIENTS AND DIRECTIONS:
Understand that a sense of urgency is the lifeblood of any entrepreneur

Develop a marathon runner's mentality

Continuously focus on goals (and deadlines), as well as your strategy and the tasks needed to achieve it

Strive to understand the need for balance between wanting things done now with the realities of the real world

BAKING AND PREP TIME:
Especially in the early stages, but certainly in difficult times

GROWTH

94% of all failure is a result of the system . . . not people. A manager of people needs to understand that all people are different. He needs to understand that the performance of anyone is governed largely by the system that he works in, the responsibility of management.
—W. EDWARDS DEMING

Our business was starting to get more complex, and we understood the necessity of developing more and better systems to run it.

The McDonald's business continued to chug along. However, the only way we could determine how McDonald's sales were doing was through conversations with the franchisee hierarchy. There was no way to know how the product was doing on the front line. This frustrated us and we decided to put in a system and infrastructure to remedy it. The first step we put in place was to visit every McDonald's we delivered to on a regular and routine basis. We hired staff whose sole responsibilities were to survey restaurants and find out how each store was performing with our product. We put together detailed scoring sheets that could measure each franchise's activity with selling muffins. We wanted to make sure that restaurants were following the correct procedures. We also needed to make sure that we knew of any potential problems and could head them off before they became bigger issues.

Going into the restaurants became an enlightening experience. We learned firsthand what the "baker" was experiencing. We learned about operational issues. We learned what the customers were saying. We were able to retrieve sales totals and the amount of wasted product. Most importantly, we got a glimpse into the McDonald's system and how they think and work. This information was invaluable and allowed us to have the confidence to expand even further.

One of the most important sales tools we began to utilize was a simple "Flux" report, a report that shows the fluctuation in units and sales dollars of our customers on a comparative basis. It was the most beneficial way for us to see comparisons with prior years, prior months, and with anything else that might be appropriate. We now had hundreds of McDonald's franchises buying our products, and this was an easy way to see if our customer simply stopped buying our products, or if they had perhaps become unhappy with our offerings. We could also see which stores were doing extremely well. Maybe they were doing something we weren't thinking about that we could share with other stores? Because we were selling all of the product directly to each McDonald's by selling to their distributor, we didn't have timely, real knowledge about the true sales activity. We were also in the dark in terms of each individual McDonald's unit. We combated that by asking the distributor to provide us with their sales data so we could put together a report on this activity and react to those findings. By being in tune with our customers' reactions to our products, we could be more proactive in growing our sales. It was painstaking and tedious work to retrieve and assemble this information, but it proved invaluable, and we would eventually apply this concept to all our business.

Many of the systems we were developing were systems that merely allowed us to survive. They were done out of necessity. Our initial basic systems centered around revenue (invoicing), sales efforts, procurement (vendor relations), production (piece rate) and employees (human resources) were rudimentary at best. But they were starting points that we continuously built upon to get to that next level. We learned a great deal about organization and systemization by being in the McDonald's system. McDonald's has one of the most successful models for promoting direction, growth, effectiveness, and stability, and for reducing or eliminating discrepancies and inconsistencies from occurring in the field. Watching how McDonald's operated and how they used systemization to oversee their franchise operation was a revelation to us. We tried, in our small way, to emulate and utilize many of the same processes we observed when we interacted with the store operations.

Our route to expansion with McDonald's was clear. They operate through regional centers. If we could be successful with one regional center, we could introduce ourselves to other centers and demonstrate what would happen if they took on our products. We presented a very good case and a successful track record. We gathered testimonials from franchisees who were using our product (usually giving them a template as to what to write). Our strategy was very similar to the strategy employed when we originally went after northeastern Ohio: find the more influential franchisees, win them over with presentations before the co-op gathering, and lay the groundwork for a successful co-op vote.

We targeted several McDonald's regions by asking our current franchisees for referrals or friends in other regions. Our first target was the Columbus, Ohio, region. We used the same blueprint as we did for northeastern Ohio: meet with as many franchisees as possible, explain the concept, and try to win them over. We were elated to eventually win the Columbus region and now realized that every McDonald's in Ohio was selling our product. Next, we went after the Pittsburgh and St. Louis regions. After those successful co-op votes, we now had more than 1,500 McDonald's franchises using our product!

Unbelievably, we were quickly getting to capacity with our new facility. We knew that at some point, we would need a larger, more modern facility, and we thus began our search. In early 1994, Akron city officials proved incredibly helpful in letting us know about any potential existing sites. For obvious reasons, they wanted us to stay in Akron, and although we didn't tell them this, we also wanted to stay there. They let us know about an industrial park they were setting up in the northernmost part of the city. To qualified parties, they were selling land for $18,000 an acre and financing it at 4 percent. We debated long and hard about making this leap to new construction with significant debt. We were at another crossroads and an important decision would need to be made.

As great as our success with McDonald's was, it wasn't without roadblocks and pitfalls. It should come as no surprise that the corporate office got involved. They weren't exactly thrilled about our methods of getting business with local franchisees. This approach, called "back-dooring," is against the McDonald's basic policy, but back then it was somewhat tolerated. Corporate came to our plant and soon requested changes to our infrastructure, including to many of our operational systems. Although it was a very difficult period of transition in our history, it was, in retrospect, a good thing. They required changes and systems that made us better and safer. We were forced to learn new concepts and approaches to production that allowed us to later procure other accounts. We grudgingly made the many changes and gradually built up some confidence with McDonald's corporate office. However, because they were used to dealing with megacompanies, we were probably one of the smallest suppliers in the system. We had our allies in the McDonald's system, but we also had many detractors. Some people in the corporate system didn't like the fact that several hundred franchises were selling product that no one else was selling and that the genesis hadn't come from the top.

While the McDonald's business was burgeoning, we started to think about selling our product to other, more traditional food service outlets. We picked three territories to target: Columbus, Pittsburgh, and Detroit. Our approach to expanding in these territories was somewhat atypical. The normal approach involved hiring food brokers, independent organizations that charge you a percentage of every sale they make. They have long and steady relationships with the distributor community and have a relatively easy time scheduling and making sales presentations. This would not have been a bad route for us except that we were a small fledgling company with no existing sales in that particular region. They would have to pioneer our product and do a lot of groundwork without knowing the future. To some, this may be exciting, but most of our efforts at persuading food brokers to take on our product line were unsuccessful. We decided to hire our own sales staff in each of these territories. This was partly due to our inability to get traditional food brokers, but also because we recognized that we would not be an important account to them. We wouldn't be their priority, nor would we be able to dictate our basic philosophies and sales strategies.

Hiring a sales staff was a very interesting learning experience. We advertised our needs in each city, requesting resumes be sent to our home office in the hopes of getting a wide range of experienced candidates. We were not disappointed. This was partly our fault, as there wasn't an accurate way to describe what we were looking for. In fact, we weren't sure what we were looking for. We screened the resumes, reducing them to ten to twelve individuals from all walks of life. Some had a lot of experience in food, and some had very little. For the most part, they were like the members of a jury pool, waiting for us to decide on their participation. We went to each city and conducted a full day's worth of interviews, not sure what to expect.

As we went through this process, we tended to gravitate toward people who shared our entrepreneurial mindset. This became more important than any food experience they may have had. Interestingly, one of the most important questions we utilized was when we asked the applicants for directions to the hotel where we would be meeting them. Back then, we didn't have all the computer mapping services that are now commonplace. A lot can be said about an individual by how they give written directions to someone. We found this to be very useful and analyzed the various responses carefully. Were the directions accurate? How much detail was included? Did they try and provide a map or was it a narrative or a bit of both? We found that the top job candidates were the people who did the best job communicating directions. It worked in reverse as well. I remember a candidate giving way too much detail. It was as if I had asked him how to find the radius of a circle and he went so far as to find the launch codes for a nuclear strike.

The process of evaluating these prospective employees was very dynamic. We could certainly hire for a variety of reasons; most of them centered around "experience." However, our approach was more amplified toward finding a new employee who would ultimately be a star performer. Nothing could replace the enthusiasm, intelligence, ambition, and excitement that exists within an inexperienced wannabe. For us, our goal was to find the diamond in the rough and guide them in the right direction.

Eventually, we settled upon individuals who really wanted to own their own business and who could benefit from the security we were offering in the way of a steady income. We wanted people who were good listeners, people who had the moxie to run their own show, and people who were aggressive and determined. We could give them autonomy and the upside of making money directly related to their efforts. We structured the relationships with the new sales team with this entrepreneurial mindset. Ultimately, we hired people from Detroit, Columbus, and Pittsburgh. This concept then allowed us to expand our food-service business, eventually adding territories in Baltimore, Washington, DC, Indianapolis, and Philadelphia. Our expansion and growth were in full motion.

In 1994, we received some good news that we had made the Inc. 500 list again. This got us some nice local press and helped fuel interest from prospective customers. No word from *Forbes*, however.

While all of this was going on, we made the bold decision to build our own facility. Working with the city of Akron, we bought four acres of land, along with an option on an additional four acres. Part of our deal with the city was that we could name the street we would reside on, since there weren't very many businesses in the industrial park. It was hard to believe. After just six years, we were ready to build our own plant! We had learned a lot in those six years, and we were eager to construct the most efficient facility possible. Although it took a lot of time and energy away from our daily grind to grow the business, we spent the necessary efforts to be able to break ground on this facility in the spring of 1994. We were going to build a 25,000-square-foot facility with ample storage, production, office, and freezer space. We couldn't fathom outgrowing this facility. The building was finished in late 1994, and we proudly moved into our new home, though I'm pretty sure our neighbors weren't very happy to have to explain all the time why their business was on Muffin Lane.

One of the accounts we continually pursued was Cracker Barrel, a very successful family restaurant chain. Unlike McDonald's, Cracker Barrel didn't have franchisees, so the only way to sell our product to them would have to be through the front door. We continually kept our name in front of them almost right after we launched the wholesale part of our business. Suddenly, their corporate office called me one day and asked if we could make streusel topping for their operations. At this point, we didn't really know what streusel topping was, let alone how to make it. Our response: "Absolutely!" Later, we would call this episode in our history, "fake and bake."

Cracker Barrel had a few other products they wanted us to look at to see if we could get one of them under our belts. They were making these products from scratch in each restaurant, and there was a concern that there were a lot of errors and inconsistencies. Could we make these products for them and streamline their operations? Well, we could certainly try. We worked very hard in developing these new products, and after a few weeks, we had prototypes ready for them to sample. Within a few more weeks, the products were in test and, soon after that, there was a national rollout. The products we developed for Cracker Barrel were based on their criteria and direct feedback. We were making it exactly the way they wanted and making the customer happy. Making a custom product was a real valuable lesson.

Like McDonald's, Cracker Barrel controlled the distribution of their own products, so we didn't have to worry about getting it to all their stores. We didn't have to worry about visiting any stores or training anyone because they already knew how to use the product; we just made it easier for them to use it. We didn't have any competition to worry about since this was "their" product and they attached a certain level of pride to it. There seemed to be a number of advantages to making a custom product for a large chain. We recognized this and made it an integral part of our ongoing sales strategy.

We accelerated our sales efforts in many directions and had numerous leads in varying stages of the sales process. Each of them had unique characteristics and undetermined sales possibilities. We were a little bit overwhelmed as to how big the future could be and no real way to measure it. We had so many questions: When would these sales come into the pipeline? Did we need to prepare for these sales? How did our potential pipeline compare to previous periods?

We started utilizing a predicative indicator tool to determine sales activity. We thought it would be a vital, helpful way to gauge our sales efforts and answer these kinds of questions. It was a very complex and exhausting process to develop, but it proved to be a staple system for running the business and gauging future capacity. We understood that, individually, our assessment of each sale would surely be inaccurate, but collectively, we were likely to get a good measurement of what the future would look like.

We also examined all of our in-process projects, handicapping their potential and assigning them numbers and probabilities. This allowed us to try and forecast what sales would occur over the next twelve months.

We understood that our individual prognosticating skills wouldn't be on target. By doing this consistently with every one of our prospects, though, we got a good measurement of future activity and were able to determine where we stood compared to past performance. Along the way, we refined our tool and sharpened the numbers. It wasn't necessarily a budget; it was a way to objectively measure our business's future potential activity.

In 1995, in large part due to our business with McDonald's and Cracker Barrel, company sales surpassed $5,000,000.

Around this same time, we decided to put together an advisory board. We were looking to garner knowledge from people with specific experience and expertise. We were very fortunate to recruit six individuals who had a cross-section of knowledge that included transportation, nutrition, production, and human resources. One of the individuals was a venture capitalist. Upon reflection, we looked at the formation of this board as one of our best ideas. We met two to three times a year, and at each meeting, we basically challenged these individuals to help us with about five issues the business was facing. The debates were lively, and the information we learned was invaluable. We received great insight from these people, which enabled us to make better decisions. Harvey and I also used the board as a way for us to mediate disagreements about which direction the business should go in or how we should handle difficult problems.

At one of our meetings, we brought up the concept of selling the business. We were continually being approached by outside suitors, and we were mulling over a particular offer we had received from a local investor. When our venture capitalist advisor heard this, he pulled us aside after the meeting and said that if we were going to sell the business, his venture firm would be extremely interested. It snowballed from there, and before you knew it, we had a letter of understanding, the document that details the terms and conditions of a sale.

A lot of thoughts and emotions were going through our minds throughout this process. Harvey and I were both married. We had started families. Most of our net worth was contained in the business. Things were going great, but there was always the potential our egg baskets could one day be crushed. After a lot of late-night discussions, we decided to move forward and sell the company to the venture firm, though we would stay on under the new ownership and build the business even bigger. Part of the deal allowed us to keep 20 percent of the new business. The buyer also wanted us to merge with a specialty fish company that imported fish from the Amazon River region. Merging us with a fish company? We didn't understand it, but what did we know about it? We thought back to the factory we had renovated a few years previously. For some reason, fate kept intertwining us with fish, even though we weren't sure what the symbolism meant.

For the most part, the investors were elated. They were slated to make more than ten times their initial investment in less than ten years. However, some of the investors weren't so happy with that return, thinking we could do even better. Those who weren't satisfied tried to derail the sale, and we spent a lot of agonizing time and energy fighting this faction off. One of those dissatisfied investors was my previously mentioned former girlfriend. It was not pretty, and tension was the order of the day. Fortunately, the votes (and control) were on our side, and we closed the transaction in the spring of 1996.

We had gone from the auction of an abandoned building to the sale of our business in less than a decade. We were ecstatic. The sales proceeds were substantial, and they enabled us to partially secure our financial future. It was the first time we had had this kind of money in our lives, and it was a great and joyful adjustment.

Things started out fine with the new ownership. They were trying to learn our business and be helpful, and they were careful not to exert too much influence . . . at least in the beginning. There was a chief executive officer (CEO) and a chief financial officer (CFO) who oversaw the two companies. They concentrated primarily on the fish business and left us alone for the most part. We let them know about a small, local cookie company that we thought would be a good acquisition candidate. After only a few months, we purchased Cambritt Cookie Company, and we were easily able to integrate them into our company. We now were heavily entrenched in cookies as well as muffins. After a few months, though, we could tell there were issues with the fish business. They were having all kinds of transportation, sales, and logistics issues. At one point, there was a prohibition placed on the fish they were importing, and they couldn't get product for a period of time.

Every week or so, there was a new crisis, and it became evident that the business was going south in a hurry. One day, the CEO called to tell us they were closing down the fish business. From here on out, they would concentrate solely on building our business. We weren't sure how to take this new approach. When the CEO told us that he and the CFO were going to be moving into our facility from the corporate offices, we started to worry. It turns out those worries were justified. The CEO took over our prized conference room, the one in between Harvey and me, where we made most of our joint decisions. Things changed rather quickly as the new owners exerted more control over "our" business. They overrode some of our decisions and made others on their own, failing to even consult us. The relationship was rapidly going downhill. Harvey and I were having emergency meetings on a regular basis. After one of them, Harvey sent me this email:

It is time we make our move. This is not fun anymore and if we don't do something now we will regret this forever. Let's meet to discuss how we leave and start something new.

It was a gut-wrenching decision, but we both knew we couldn't go on like this. We had to force a change. After a subsequent late-night discussion over cigars and beers, we decided we would leave. We didn't know what we would do, but we were confident we could find a better place and something that would bring back our passion. The next morning, we went into the CEO's office and told him we were both going to be leaving. It was time for a change, though we said we would stay if it would help smooth the transition. He didn't try to convince us or dig deeper into our decision. It was all over in a matter of fifteen minutes, and we left the meeting exhilarated about what the future might hold, even though we had no idea what to expect next.

It wasn't long before the CEO told the venture firm what had happened, and they began plotting their strategy for our exit. The next day, we got a call from one of the venture firm's partners, asking if he could meet with us. A subsequent meeting was arranged later that afternoon, and when it happened, he got right down to business.

"So, you want to leave," he said.

"Yes, it just isn't what we expected," we countered.

"What would it take for you to stay?" he responded.

We never expected that question. What would it take for us to stay? We hadn't contemplated that. We had just assumed it wasn't an option. Harvey and I looked at each other, not sure what the other was thinking, but we both instinctively knew the answer.

"We would stay . . . if . . . they would leave . . . and we would be ones to build the business," we put forth, hesitantly, but with pride.

He nodded his head in seeming acceptance and told us that he would think about it and get back to us the next day. Our heads were spinning. We had gone from being ready to pack up our offices to possibly being back in charge, building the business to new heights.

Harvey and I huddled after the meeting, contemplating everything that was said and trying to prognosticate what would happen. It was exciting to think about it, but we were careful not to get carried away with a possible decision we had no control over. True to his word, the partner called us the next day and told us that if we wanted to stay, the company would be restructured and we would be the new CEOs. The existing regime would be let go. Our emotions were running wild. There was some guilt about their departure but also a lot of exhilaration about the future.

Over the next few weeks, the former CEO and CFO packed up their belongings and started the transition of control back to us. In our view, it was an amazing turn of events and our outlook changed tremendously. We also got our conference room back. This new outlook not only included running the business, but it was also incumbent upon us to plan the purchase of other complementary businesses. We needed to grow at a fast pace to satisfy the venture firm's appetite.

As we started this new process, we soon learned the ramifications of the fish business's demise. We also learned about the lucrative severance arrangements the former CEO and CFO had. They would continue to receive all of their executive benefits and salary for several more months. No wonder they weren't too critical about leaving the company—"Sure, I'll agree to a very, very long vacation with full pay . . . when do I leave?" We also determined the scope of the financial impact that the fish business had on our business. Their financing and negative cash flow had fatigued our financial strength, and we were highly leveraged. The fish business had been a dream project of the investors, but it had required a lot of infrastructure costs and working capital to get up and running. Unfortunately, it took a lot of time to get up to the point of "almost running" before they realized it wouldn't succeed. We would be the ones to inherit the aftermath and pick up the pieces. We began to retool our mindsets, trying to figure out how to get back on track.

We started to examine what made us successful with sales prospects. Who was our ideal customer? We began to develop a framework for determining who our top prospects should be. We took a step back and analyzed our most successful accounts and determined what was consistent about each of them. Did they have certain attributes we could identify? Maybe they all had a geographic connection? Maybe they shared the way they made decisions? Looking for trends and particularities, we identified about fifteen attributes of these accounts and assigned different point values to each of them. We knew we were on the right track because our current top accounts had high scores. It took us a long time to harness the right approach. We constantly refined, adjusted, and changed things, but the time spent on this process was well worth it. Once we had defined our attributes and determined a scoring system, we could now start to apply them to prospects.

We next began the necessary process of researching and scoring prospects. Again, this wasn't easy. We had to be both creative and persistent in gathering this data. We found that simply calling the prospect and asking them the necessary questions worked best. We were careful not to try and "sell them" during the call. The prospect needed to know that we were merely gathering information. This approach usually resulted in them being more forthcoming with useful information. After our research was complete, we started to score our prospects, trying to determine where we could best marshal our resources to plot a comprehensive strategy that targeted these accounts.

We felt very confident that these prospects would be ideal accounts. They would remain on our target list forever until they either became an account or, because of some new revelation, ceased to be ideal. This was an important mindset for us to have. We took this approach that we wouldn't give up and that our persistence would eventually win the day. For most sales-minded individuals, this is a crucial paradigm shift, and it takes some time to get used to. The sales prognosticator tool became an important instrument in our overall sales process. It helped us understand the value of being able to focus on a prospect list that was fairly small and consistent. Why should we spend the time, energy, and resources on the bottom prospects when we could be going for the cream of the crop?

....

Muffin Recipe #5:
A Systemization Mindset

INGREDIENTS AND DIRECTIONS:
Think of your business as a franchisor that needs to develop systems for its franchisees

Use systemization to foster direction, stability, effectiveness, consistency, and growth

Learn from the ways other companies use systems

Develop systems for the company with the mindset that it will succeed without the entrepreneur's intricate involvement

BAKING AND PREP TIME:
Start early and add layers as you go

Unfinished Building at 214 S. Main St., 1985

Finished Building at 214 S. Main St., 1987

Our First Delivery Vehicle, 1992

Former Fish Plant Turned Muffin Plant, 1992

1994

Senator John Glenn with Me and My Son,
Wyatt, 1992

President Clinton with Muffin Men, 1993

Henry Kissinger with Me before Getting Angry, 1994

Main Street Gourmet's Current Plant, 2018

Main Street Gourmet Logo

THE HEAT
OF THE BATTLE

Razors need a hard, gritty, and arduous path to get sharpened and be a strong instrument. So do entrepreneurs.

—STEVE MARKS

Soon after our "takeover," our McDonald's business arrangement began to show signs of deterioration. The corporate office began to exert its influence and got involved in many of the mundane issues. We started to hear feedback that the restaurants were unable to keep pace with the muffin sales, given the fact that the biscuit oven was being used for other products. The restaurant workers' time was being stretched, and people were questioning the importance and rationale for making fresh-baked muffins.

Eventually, we were asked if we could simplify the process, making it even easier than the "defrost, scoop out, and bake" formula we had come up with. We went to work and developed a concept that use pre-deposited muffin batter in aluminum foil pans. The restaurants could take this product from the freezer to the oven and have a fresh-baked muffin without much labor and with no pans to clean. The product wasn't quite as good as the original (we had to reformulate it to allow it to be baked from a frozen state), but the ease of use became more important, and eventually, over the course of about six months, it became the standard. This change caused an upheaval to our system, but it made us better and more versatile. But we had to ask ourselves if we were sacrificing quality for profits. Had we sold our soul? Was the customer always right?

The McDonald's corporate office continued its pattern of becoming more involved in the process, and along the way, we began to lose some restaurants. Typically, we were told that the product just didn't warrant the attention or that, given the demands of a McDonald's employee, it was still too difficult to prepare. For the first time, we were trying to hold on to business instead of building it up. We became nervous each time McDonald's called. That nervousness would later be justified.

Now that we were in control and reporting directly to the venture firm, we started the process of pursuing acquisitions. One company that caught our attention was a small company called Isabella's. They were located in Providence, Rhode Island, and they sold sugar-free and fat-free muffins to supermarkets in the New York City, New England, and mid-Atlantic regions. Up to this point, we had never made finished, baked products. If we could purchase a company like Isabella's, we could get into the "baking" business and expand from our batters and doughs. This acquisition made a lot of sense on several different fronts. For one, the banks were more likely to loan us funds for existing cash flow versus the alternative of starting a baking operation from the ground up. Secondly, the business was concentrated in a territory and business segment that didn't overlap with our existing situation. Lastly, Isabella's had annual sales of about $2.5 million, which meant it was small enough for us to acquire while still having a lot of upside. The venture firm was on board with the idea, and we moved forward with the acquisition, completing it in the spring of 1999.

After analyzing their business, it became clear that we could be much more efficient with a new plant. Rather than build a new one, we decided to expand our existing one in Akron and add a baking function. We would move Isabella's from Providence into our expanded facility while keeping a sales function out East. During the summer of 1999, we began plans to expand our building with an additional 35,000 square feet of space. Our total cost to expand the plant, move Isabella's, and be prepared to bake product would be about $2 million. It was an expensive but logical path forward. Our venture firm funded additional equity into our company, and we borrowed more money from the bank. In the late spring of 2000, we moved Isabella's to Akron, which was—and it looked this way to our customers—a seamless transition.

During 1999, my wife, Jeannine, and I started a family foundation to benefit local charities. The way people usually do this is by simply donating investment proceeds to charity. But another more intriguing option for us was to try and create something from nothing. We looked at the X Games, the Gravity Games, and events of this nature. Jeannine and I had both run more than twenty marathons each, and we wondered why Akron didn't have one. We thought, "Why couldn't little Akron, Ohio, develop a world-class marathon?" But the other part of my brain was saying, "Do we really need to take on something new and difficult?"

One of my favorite marathon memories involves the Boston Marathon. Jeannine and I ran the race with 21,000 other people in eighty-seven-degree heat. The gun went off . . . we waited twenty minutes before even moving . . . and we eventually crossed the start line twenty-seven minutes later. I was already kind of tired at that point. I did manage to run a pretty good race and made it to mile twenty-four before I started to fade. Within about a half mile of the finish line, I was barely able to move forward. It happened—what marathon runners call "the wall." I looked to my right. A man was attempting to pass me wearing a shirt that read, "80 and still running." I was in my early forties then. How would you have reacted? I am not sure about you, but I was not about to let this eighty-year-old man pass me. I became possessed and chased after this octogenarian. As I started to catch up with him, I began thinking, "What am I doing? What kind of accomplishment is this?" I backed off and let him beat me. At least that's my official version of events. Truthfully, I couldn't catch him! It was a humbling experience to say the least.

A marathon race is special. It's a unique community occasion, a bold event that challenges our sense of what we as individuals can achieve. It is different than any other endurance event because participants are ordinary people who are doing something extraordinary. These are people who have challenged themselves in the realization of a dream. They have pushed themselves to the threshold, training for many weeks and months, pursuing a goal that very few people can accomplish. They are an inspiration to the entire community by creating a spirit of optimism, achievement, and success.

If you have ever run a marathon, or even if you've watched from the sidelines, you know what I am talking about and what I mean by the spirit of the event. You know how spectators embrace a marathon that goes through their community. People come out of their homes and cheer on the runners. They pass out refreshments, bands play music, and it's just a festive atmosphere that is hard to duplicate.

If you look at the barriers to entry of developing such an event, you need money, community support, and government backing. Our foundation had the money, and we were very confident that the community would support the endeavor, but we ultimately needed the local government to be on board. I went to James Phelps, Akron's deputy mayor for economic development, and ultimately to Mayor Don Plusquellic with some questions. Would the city support and nurture such an endeavor? How could we accomplish everything that would need to be done? Without much hesitation, they both indicated they would partner with us.

This episode in my life could be filed under the heading "Be Careful What You Wish For." After the city signed on, I had the same feeling I had when I walked out of that building on Main Street with my father. What had I gotten myself into? I already had a full-time job!

Like starting any new business, when organizing for the marathon got underway, I did the normal things. From the beginning, I underestimated everything that would need to be done. I sought out advice from community leaders to make sure that I could gain their support and elicit valuable advice. Their feedback became the litmus test, and we decided to move forward. Fortunately, I also had the benefit of my previous business experience and could lay out the most efficient timeline and groundwork for a successful event. We set the inaugural race for October 2003, more than two years away.

Like any new business, we created our mission statement:

Provide a World Class Marathon that would galvanize the community, promote health and fitness, stimulate the local economy, bring national attention to the region, and benefit charitable organizations.

We began the brainstorming process, meeting with consultants and a small volunteer base to develop our goals and aspirations. We came up with budgets, business and marketing plans, and organizational charts. I quickly realized that the management of the marathon was not something I could do while still being part of Main Street Gourmet. So I soon hired an executive race director and an operations director. I also formed functional and necessary committees, including ones for marketing, traffic control, runner safety, registration, course selection, water stations, and runner transportation.

We reached out to our business community for initial sponsorships and were able to get many prominent sponsors, which secured a financially successful event. The snowball was rolling.

We debated and brainstormed about what would give us the level of credibility to be on par with the best marathons in the world. Who was the best-known distance runner in the world? One name kept coming up—four-time winner of the Boston Marathon and four-time winner of the New York Marathon, Olympian Bill Rodgers. We ultimately hired Bill to be our national spokesperson, to be our consultant, and to run in the race. His presence instantly legitimized our event.

We knew we needed to understand the business of running a marathon, so we reached out to the Cincinnati and Pittsburgh Marathons and benchmarked with them. We looked at best practices from other marathons as well: Boston, Chicago, the Twin Cities, and New York.

Next, we looked at the course. Ideally, you want a marathon course to be flat, which obviously makes it better for runners. This was difficult in Akron given the hilly terrain. We also wanted the course to be special and to pass by many of our great landmarks. That was easier to accomplish. We came up with the idea to join forces with USA Track & Field (USATF) and create a USATF-sanctioned challenge race between the United States, Mexico, and Canada, whereby each of those countries would select their five best runners to form a team to compete for prize money and bragging rights. The Marathon Relay Championships of North America was born.

We did some other unique things with our race as well. Instead of just printing the traditional number on the racing bib, we used people's first names. That way, when a runner went through a neighborhood, spectators could say, "Way to go, Bill," instead of "Way to go, 354." We also included entertainment on the course. Along the race route, we set up more than twenty-five bands and other forms of entertainment at every possible area. Music and fun became a focal point throughout the course, spurring runners on. We contracted with comedian and then *Tonight Show* host Jay Leno to headline a postrace concert, and that created a buzz. The negotiation with his people was fun. Never in my lifetime did I think I would be mediating issues like private jets, jet fuel costs, and dressing room frills.

On October 3, 2003, on a picture-perfect Saturday morning, the Akron Marathon was launched. In that first year, a total of 3,775 runners participated in either the full 26.2-mile marathon or the five-person relay. More than 3,000 volunteers attended to the mountain of details that would impress runners and bring them back to Akron again. Today, the Akron Marathon annually hosts over 20,000 participants as part of the Summa Health Akron Marathon Race Series with a full-time staff headed by Anne Bitong (a former employee of Main Street Gourmet).

This experience left me with a lot of good feelings and a valuable lesson about community involvement, but I still had a full-time job and a lot of other responsibilities to attend to.

The equity infusion to buy Isabella's—and an earlier one to stem the red ink from the debacle with the fish business—diluted the financial interest of the original shareholders from their original 20 percent to less than 2 percent. We had no real control over the structure, and therefore, they could call the shots on how our shares would be diluted. They still owed us a considerable amount of money from the sale of the company, so we were still very motivated to make sure the company was successful. However, our dilution taught us a very valuable lesson. When you're an entrepreneur and you don't have real control, your mindset changes and you don't have the same feeling going to work each day. Harvey and I learned to live with this feeling because there was still a lot at stake. Plus, our families and employees were counting on us. Our sales were approaching $12 million.

We received yet another ominous call from McDonald's, wanting to know if we could now make a finished muffin that the restaurants could just "thaw and serve." Making muffins was just too difficult a process given everything else they did. We began the ugly transition of moving restaurants from making fresh-baked muffins to using a product that merely required someone to take it out of the freezer and thaw it. I think you know where this is headed.

The changeover took about six months to complete, and predictably, we started to get complaints.

"These muffins aren't as good," was the usual criticism.

"We know," was our typical reply.

Our hands were tied. The McDonald's corporate office got their way, but gradually, sales declined. A few months later, we got word that the St. Louis region was dropping muffins altogether due to the low sales. A few weeks later, another region called to say they were discontinuing the product. By the end of 2002, we only had about 150 McDonald's franchises buying our product.

A customer may be wrong about what is good or bad, but they are always right about what they think is good or bad.

—STEVE MARKS

I started to realize that adversity was a common thread throughout my entrepreneurial journey. No one has built a successful business without coming to grips with adversity's many facets. I learned that I would not be successful by only doing enjoyable endeavors. That just wasn't realistic. The best entrepreneurs are the ones who can anticipate and handle the unavoidable challenges facing them without derailing their passion. Tackling adversity would be a building block enabling all of us to build strength, new muscle that could be utilized for the next hurdle. It would be our approach and response to adversity that would determine our fate.

McDonald's sales represented about 15 percent of our business. Harvey and I were continually cheering each other up when one of us seemed down. We were trying to promote a positive attitude, but it was still hard. Losing most of our business with McDonald's was a very difficult time for us. At the same time, our "entrepreneurial" sales regions were facing hurdles as well. Many of the small distributors that we were selling to were either going out of business or being bought out by large national distributors who did not carry our product.

However, a significant amount of our business was selling to the rebels of the chains. For example, we sold to a JW Marriot Hotel on the East Coast. Technically, they were required to buy a certain muffin from a certain company—what the industry would call a "hard spec." Because we had a relationship with this hotel, though, and because they opted for a higher quality product, we enjoyed the business. As time went on, many of these chains were forcing their individual outlets to buy only the products that they had a hard spec on; in essence, no more ordering off of the menu. For really the first time in our history, we were faced with a downturn in sales. We had to make cutbacks and it was painful. We also had to rework our strategy and vision to determine a better course of action.

After extensive discussion, analysis, and heartache, we developed a focused strategy, a real necessity if we were going to survive, let alone thrive. We weren't going to let circumstances dictate to us what we should do. We were going to make a bold move; we would concentrate our efforts by putting most of our resources into the concept of developing custom products for chains. Large chains control distribution: they tell the distributor to carry the product. We didn't have the power of a Pillsbury, with their infrastructure, advertising, and marketing. Therefore, we couldn't compete against them using traditional tactics. We knew we would lose battles with the industry giants in conventional sales settings. Companies like Pillsbury are formidable competitors. But making a custom product leveled the playing field. We could turn the product around faster. We could also run small batches and wouldn't have to worry about utilizing vast equipment and assembly lines. We could be flexible, responsive, and attentive. Maybe David could beat Goliath.

We needed the large chains to wield power for us and pave the way for distribution. Also, distributors are "encouraged" to pay you on time. Otherwise, the customer is likely to forestall their next order. The distributors desperately need to make sure they receive product or they simply can't sell it. We had the leverage. The venture firm agreed with our strategy and we made the appropriate changes to our business.

These were not small changes in either philosophy or structure. Our changes involved a multitude of strategic initiatives, including paying less attention (and devoting fewer resources) to our food service business. At the time, our food service business, stock product sold through distributors to restaurants and other food establishments, comprised most of our revenue. We had to change our production methods and purchase additional equipment in order to have more capability. It was a delicate balancing act. Because the food service business was the portion of the company that paid the bills, we couldn't just ignore it.

Part of the transition involved converting most of our regional sales representatives into independent contractors, which, in effect, made them food brokers by putting them on commission instead of a standard salary. Many people's livelihoods were impacted, and it was an uphill battle to make this plan happen, but it ultimately benefited all our employees in the long run.

We limped along with this strategy, losing food service business and replacing it with custom business, but we weren't growing significantly. We knew we were on the right track, but we also knew it would take time.

The venture firm was not as inclined to be so patient. By 2003, they had been in this investment for more than seven years—a long time by venture firm standards—and they were interested in quicker results. During the summer of 2004, they told us that they had made a large investment in one of our competitors. *Wow, great,* we thought. They also told us that it didn't make sense to integrate us into that competitor and that they would be putting us up for sale. *Even better.* They wanted to know if were interested in buying the business back. *Okay, now this is getting interesting!*

We started putting the pieces together for a deal to buy the business back. We would have to put in very little money, and we would only have to restructure some of the existing loans. We often were tempted to treat the purchase of the business like a poker game. Like a good card game, the cast of characters and their bluffing attributes are a major part of the experience. Privately, we were very anxious and committed to buying the business back, and we struggled to hold back our excitement. During our negotiations with the venture firm, we often found ourselves at decision points, when we would tell our attorney, Jeff Leonard, "Either they do this, or we walk."

"Are you sure that's what you want?" he would respond. "Don't bluff. You must be prepared to do what you say, otherwise your claims and decisions will have little consequence and muster," he would add. He was right! Sometimes we would back down and other times we wouldn't, but our litmus test always came back to this question: "Would we walk away?"

We knew we were in a position of strength; we had a good poker hand. We made it very well-known to them that if someone other than us was going to own the business, we were likely to leave. It was understood that if we left the business, the relationships that we had forged with customers would be gone. Our employees would have diminished loyalty and less security. It would be a lengthy learning curve for someone new to manage the business. Bottom line, we were the best potential buyers and we had the best hand. They knew it and we knew it. We also knew that the venture firm's investment in our business was a nuisance and that they had to get out of it; their hand just wasn't worth it. Their only real concern was making sure that they got the best deal for their shareholders and that it didn't look like we stole the business.

We made a lowball bid and waited. They countered with something significantly higher. It was at this time that we opted to

just say "no thank you" instead of "come back with a counteroffer."
We were willing to walk. After several days, they came back to us
with an offer higher than our original one but much closer to it. We
had several choices. Accept it, say "no thank you" again, or counter.
We opted to counter again but with the understanding that we were
done negotiating. We were prepared to walk away, and they knew we
weren't bluffing. We really wanted to have the business back again,
and we were on edge, waiting for their response.

They accepted, and we consummated the sale on August 4, 2004.
I am sure they evaluated all the possibilities and realized the risk of
refusing our latest offer. We were able to buy the business back at a
price we wanted, and all of it was traceable back to the idea of getting
them to wonder if we would walk away or not. Negotiations almost
certainly don't follow this script all the time, but we knew our limits
and the poker hand we held, and we knew our opponent. That was
the key to walking away with the chips.

All of a sudden, it started to become fun again. Harvey and I
spent several hours mulling over the possibilities and getting very
excited about the future. We could be entrepreneurs again!

We had one particular problem that kept nagging us, though.
While we had a pretty good rate of producing products to the
specifications customers outlined, occasionally, the finished
products came out imperfectly. The flaws may have been entirely
aesthetic—too brown, too light, too sweet, not sweet enough—or
that the recipe hadn't been followed accurately—too much sugar
or not enough. Depending on how salvageable it was, we would
either throw the product away or donate it to local charities, like
our local Akron-Canton Foodbank. Even though the amount of
"faulty" production made up a relatively low percentage of our
whole production, it started to add up to significant dollars over time.

Harvey and I needed to think of a solution that could recoup that money and add to our bottom line.

During a brainstorming meeting, we came up with the idea of selling the imperfect product to the public at a discount and donating a percentage of the proceeds to local charities. Over a year's time, we would accumulate the imperfect product in our freezer and have a massive one-day sale that could potentially go on to become a yearly tradition. We would call it the "No Muffin Left Behind" sale—sort of a tongue-in-cheek homage to the 2002 Congressional act aimed at helping disadvantaged students. Everything would be sold for $1 per pound. It would come in the same packaging—ten to thirty-pound cases—that we sold to our wholesale customers. Despite some minimal advertising, we had no idea how much product we could sell or if anyone would even show up. It had been a while since our storefront days selling to individual customers.

So, in the spring of 2004, on one beautiful Saturday, I arrived at the plant a few hours before the start of the sale, totally not knowing what to expect. As I approached our facility, a swarm of cars filled the normally empty weekend streets. The sidewalks looked like a street carnival, and people were milling about in lawn chairs, chatting with others. I couldn't believe what I was witnessing; hundreds of people in line before dawn, patiently waiting at our dock doors for the sale to start! Before I could indulge in the excitement that all these people were there for our sale, I thought, "Wait. Did I miss something? Was Bruce Springsteen scheduled to appear at some point?"

I moved toward the line to see if I could make out a conversation or somehow visually investigate the crowd's purpose for being here. Eventually, I approached a few people and started probing. *Why are you here so early? What do you hope to find? When does Bruce Springsteen go on?* The answers were all in our favor—this was an opportunity to stock up on Main Street Gourmet product. Since our product, with our name representing it, wasn't available to the public, most of the people in line were customers from our early days at the Main Street storefront. Fortunately, we had dozens of employees on hand who were ready to volunteer their time to help some loyal customers and raise money for a good cause. The day was a blur of unexpected triumph and exciting new territory. As word spread throughout the area, the lines stayed long for the entirety of the sale.

People loved the uncommon and distinctive characteristics of these baked good "mistakes": blueberry muffins with way more than a sprinkle of sugar covering the top, chocolate chip cookies that used milk chocolate chips instead of semi-sweet, a caramel brownie with more caramel than brownie, and a plethora of other combinations.

The sale ended at 1:00 p.m. We loaded up the truck with what was left from the sale and sent it to the Akron-Canton Foodbank. It was a great day, and it opened up an opportunity for us to redirect much of our previously wasted product by selling it while simultaneously helping local charities. That particular sale helped fund travel expenses for our employee, John Calaway, on his trip to participate as a speed skater in the 2005 Special Olympics in Nagano, Japan. John ended up returning home with two gold medals and one bronze! We would go on to have semiannual "No Muffin Left Behind" sales, and because of its growing popularity, space requirements led us to eventually move the sale to the Akron-Canton Foodbank's facility.

As 2004 was ending, we now had a business that was doing $13 million per year. When we sold it, we had been doing $6 million per year. We continued to add larger, more reputable food establishment accounts. Our strategy of focusing on national and regional custom accounts was starting to pay off. We continued to adapt our facility to this philosophy, and the opportunities seem plentiful. Sales bounced above $15 million in 2005, making it our most profitable year yet. The bounce was also back in our step, and it was fun to go to work again.

Gaining our business back changed our philosophy, priorities, and approach. We weren't worried about satisfying investors or growing just to have an exit strategy. We started to target accounts that were good matches for us. One account we targeted was a fledgling natural food grocery chain called Wild Oats. We worked very hard to try and procure this account and settled on an approach that eliminated SKUs (SKUs are "stock-keeping units" or items in inventory). They were buying dozens of different muffin batters from different suppliers. We pitched the concept of supplying them with six to eight base batters (including basic, bran, low fat, corn, vegan, and whole wheat) so that each location could develop their own concoctions by adding unique products at the store level.

We developed five recipe suggestions for each base batter to get them started. This concept became the cornerstone of a solid relationship. It was truly a problem-solver for the customer (reducing space, cost, and SKUs) while providing them with creative capabilities and advantages over their competitors. Now that we had proved ourselves with the base batters, we suggested other products to solve a problem or improve their quality. Also, by selling them more products, we could ship larger quantities and be more efficient with pricing and freight. Obviously, we were quick to communicate this situation to them, and they understood the implications. Slowly and systematically, we became one of their leading bakery suppliers, supplying them with dozens of different products. Wild Oats, though they only supplied twenty or so stores in the Colorado region, soon became our second largest customer.

We weren't always successful with every prospect. For example, at one point, we were in the final stages of finding out if a prospect was going to buy our product—a custom cookie for a midsize, national chain. It was a very large account, one that would be very important to our growth. Several months had been spent wooing the prospect. A price was on the table, and we were waiting for a response. The week when we were supposed to get a decision came and went without a word, so we called the customer and found out that they were struggling with their decision about whether to go with an incumbent supplier or with us. The decision was tough; they appreciated all our hard work but needed more time to give a final answer. While we could certainly respect that, we stewed. We started second-guessing ourselves, trying to determine what we could do to tip the scales.

After playing mind games with myself, I started to think we weren't going to win the business. I decided to look at the pricing again to see if there was any room for a reduction. To my surprise, a few raw materials had gone down in market price since our first quote, meaning we could cut about 5 percent and still maintain our standard gross profit margin. I reasoned that if the prospect was debating switching to us, a price reduction of this magnitude, which would save the prospect several hundred thousand dollars through the course of the year, would surely tip the scales.

I pushed our sales team to react. We crafted an email explaining our position and offered a new price. I was relieved after making that move and felt we did all we could—a job well done. A few days later, we got the call from the prospect informing us that the incumbent would get the business. Astonishingly, our price maneuver worked against us. The prospect said this ninth-inning tactic was unprofessional and could not be condoned. Our email was viewed completely differently than we had intended.

Email, with all its simplicity and efficiency, had and still has its faults, like all digital means of communication. It can't convey the whole message—the right tone, emotion, and intent. Our email was seen as an act of desperation.

I took this very personally and reflected on the situation. I wondered what we should have done differently. I think the biggest mistake was not talking directly to the prospect about the price change. We could have probed the prospect a bit about the decision, asked if price was a factor, or if there was anything else we could have done to win the business.

In retrospect, the email was impersonal and could have been read a bunch of different ways. Even though it was extremely difficult to get the prospect on the phone, we should have persevered in that direction. However, I am still amazed at the prospect's reaction. One thing is for sure, you just never know what someone is thinking. I also was a little confused about why I was taking it so personally. I've always had a problem with that, and I knew it was something I would continually have to work on. Michael Corleone said it best: "It's not personal, it's strictly business." If I could only believe that.

As we got more and more experience with procuring accounts, we started to understand how paramount loyal customers were to our success. Along the way, we lost some accounts for a variety of reasons—they went out of business, they discontinued the product we were providing, they switched to a competitor. When you obtain a loyal customer, it's basically like an annuity, a hugely important aspect of growing a business. One tried-and-true sales tenet that has stood the test of time is that "the easiest sale you can make is to your current customers." That needs to be remembered. Obtaining a new customer is extremely difficult, and the process can be fraught with land mines. One situation exemplifies this. A potential customer asked us for a quote on a product that one of our competitors was producing for them. We were told that we would get the business if our pricing was competitive. It was shaping up to be a very large sale and we were foaming at the mouth. The customer gave us the recipe and asked how much we would charge to make it. After analyzing the recipe, it was clear we could make the product considerably cheaper than what they were paying. We also knew we could win on price because they had accidentally sent us a bill that showed what our competitor was charging them.

Having the bill in hand created a bit of a dilemma. The debate began internally about whether to quote an amount slightly less than what they were paying or to quote our standard gross margin pricing. If we quoted our standard margin, we would be forgoing several tens of thousands of dollars. If we quoted a price just below what the customer was paying, we would maximize our profits.

On the surface, maximizing profits seemed to be the obvious decision. Or was it? We began to ask ourselves why we were getting the chance to quote this product. Maybe the prospect realized that they were being gouged. After all, they had the recipe and they undoubtedly had an idea concerning the cost to produce it. How would it look to them if we came in with a price just below what they were paying? What if we instead came in with a price that blew them away? We decided to go with the lowest price and try to be the customer's vendor for a long time. Lucky for us, it was the right choice.

Greed, we discovered, was why our competitor lost the business and why we had the chance to take it over. That customer is currently one of our largest, accounting for millions of dollars in annual sales. Had we been shortsighted, we would have ultimately lost out on long-term profits. We learned not to let greed kill what can be a far more lucrative relationship from a loyal, trusting customer.

In 2007, we received some alarming news. Whole Foods, the

leading natural foods chain, was going to be buying Wild Oats. *Ugh.* We didn't supply Whole Foods, and if previous history was any indication, Whole Foods would gobble up Wild Oats and convert everything over to their system, which meant we could potentially lose our second-largest account in one fell swoop. There was little we could do until the transaction was complete. No one knew what would ultimately happen, and no one wanted to make any commitments. Our only hope was that the US Justice Department would not approve the deal. But after a few months, they did, and our worries manifested into realities.

Now that the die was cast, we had to develop a plan to save this business. We determined that the Wild Oats stores were going to be converted to Whole Foods, becoming part of its Colorado region. Our strategy was to convince the new regime that our products should stay in this region since they were so successful, but we had to convince them all over again. There was a lot of confusion over the transition, and they weren't in the mood to make significant changes. This played into our hands, and when the day came to make our presentation to the region's leadership team, we made a passionate argument that our product had a loyal following, was cost-effective, and that its demise would only result in a loss of goodwill and a rise in customer disappointment. They understood this angle, and with minimal deliberation, they agreed that our products should stay. We were overjoyed with relief and quickly realized (on the flight home) that this turn of events became a significant strength for us. Not only were we retaining the business, but now we were an approved Whole Foods vendor and had our products in their system! Now we just needed a plan of attack to go after other regions.

Approved products in the Whole Foods System became a "hunting license." We could now go out and call on all the Whole

Foods regional bakery managers and let them know the products we currently provided. While we were communicating this, we would also convey our capabilities for other products. It became a great sales strategy. We were able to probe into their needs and react accordingly. We gradually added new products to match these needs. Each new product we added could be pitched to the other regions. Soon, our product catalog quickly reached dozens of products in their system, resulting in millions of dollars of sales and a new top customer.

As we added new products, we also built our capability. One day, our sales director, Nate Searles, brought an interesting opportunity to us. The bakery director at Wild Oats had left the company, but we had kept in touch with him. This communication would prove to be very valuable and rewarding. He ended up taking a job as head of the soup division at a prominent fast-casual concept. This prospect was a dream account for us and pretty much for everyone in the bakery business. While we certainly didn't have any capability with soup, we made a point of "tracking down" former contacts to see where they had landed. This person was a fan of our company and offered to put us in touch with his new company's bakery division. He even offered to give us a recommendation.

We were eventually introduced to the bakery director. After the typical song and dance routine with the sales presentation, we were asked if we had capability to do granola. While we had never really made granola before, we weren't going to let inexperience be a factor for us.

"Of course, we can make granola," we told them.

Once again, our bravado known as "fake and bake," which we'd first used during the Cracker Barrel streusel development, was being put back into circulation.

We feverishly worked toward figuring out the normal process for making granola, and then we tried to determine if we could make the product within our facility. As it turned out, we could do it! After adapting our equipment and processes, we determined a method for making granola and ultimately submitted samples for their approval. After several weeks and multiple ideations, a product was approved! Now that we had a solid process of making granola, we circled back to Whole Foods and our other accounts to see if we could sell more products to our existing customers—a basic tenet of any sales organization. Granola became a real boon to our business, a new category that was growing by leaps and bounds. Company sales exceeded $20 million, and we felt a new confidence that hadn't existed before. We began to add people in areas we couldn't previously afford to, and we started to look at correcting bottlenecks and weaknesses.

Successfully obtaining this account actually related back to the fact that we had kept in contact with the former bakery director at Wild Oats. This revelation prompted us to make it a policy to have our salespeople keep all their relationships connected, even if someone wasn't a customer. Before getting this account, we really didn't understand and consider the importance of this. If we were doing our job, we should have built up trust, respect, and confidence with that customer. Any time an integral employee left our customer, our salespeople knew the drill. Find out where the person had landed and what the situation was. Once we connected with that person, we had a lot of information to explore. Did he or she find a new job and if so, was it in the same industry? Was there any insight into the customer that they were willing to divulge? Certainly, if the person was working in the same industry, we would have a potential pipeline for new business. Often, this would lead to a very viable prospect. If the person didn't have a job, we would offer to help them find new employment. And if we were successful, we would have a devoted friend for life.

We continued to focus on custom foods, adding new processes, including double-baked products (products that require them to be baked, removed from the oven, and then eventually baked again). While this process made it more difficult for our production team, it gave us an edge over our competitors and endeared us to more customers who didn't want to add this burden to their operations. Our sales continued their climb, surpassing the $23 million mark. The future looked very bright.

It was at this time that we started to think about our exit strategy and process. We had been down this road before, and we determined that if we ever did it again, we'd do it right. You may be asking, why would we want to sell when business was going so well? Back in 1996, we really sold the company to diversify our wealth and to have someone help us get to that next level. Now, we were in our early fifties and we were beginning to think about retirement. We each had three kids who were either too young to take over the business or uninterested in doing so. Selling now would set up the landscape for the next ten to fifteen years. We started the conversation with our advisors and outside parties. Once you make this move, it is hard to pull back, and the inertia was soon rolling beyond our control.

In the fall of 2010, we started to talk to investment bankers, and we became more entrenched with the thought of divesting a significant stake in our company. We settled upon an investment banking firm to represent us and began the unwieldy process of assembling data, developing strategy, and formulating a comprehensive list of potential suitors. The process had started, and there was no turning back. We decided not to tell anyone in the company except for a few people who had to know in order to retrieve data. It was hard and ugly; every day was filled with tension as we assembled more and more data in order to put together the "book" that would be the principal document by which organizations would initially evaluate us.

A real secret is something which only one person knows.
—INDRIES SHAH

In early December 2010, we were ready to send the book to about twenty organizations that had responded to a "teaser" letter (they didn't yet know that we were the company for sale), along with a confidentiality agreement. The next phase had started, and the stress and pressure escalated. After many discussions, about eight organizations submitted bids for our evaluation. The bids were all over the place, not only in terms of money, but also structure. We narrowed it down to four organizations that we would allow to come in for management presentations beginning in early January 2011. The presentations were grueling and painstaking. Very few stones were left unturned. We had a great story to tell, and our future looked bright. However, they were all looking for negative issues that would ultimately affect the price.

After a long day, the visiting group would usually go out with us to a nice restaurant with the aim of getting to know us a bit better. We were trying to do the same to determine if we could work with them going forward. Near the end of January, having completed the last presentation, we sat down, trying to gauge all the data and our interactions with our future partners. During this process, a small investment firm contacted our investment banker, wondering if they could still get in on the action and place a bid. After some discussion, we reluctantly agreed to hear their offer if it could be done very quickly. Within a day or so, they came back with a very competitive bid. It also included many creative elements, including no escrow and allowing us to keep the real estate. We became intrigued. Who were these guys? "These guys" ended up being two thirty-something businessmen who were just starting out on their own. We would be their first investment. Their bid wasn't the highest, but it was definitely in the game.

After meeting with our investment banker, we decided that there were three companies we wanted to earnestly negotiate with. One of the companies was a classic New York investment firm. They had made the top offer and one of the investments in their portfolio was a competitor of ours, so they seemed to know our business very well. The discussions intensified, and we only heard bits and pieces along the way, which was good because the process was distracting enough. When the dust settled, the New York private equity firm was somewhat ahead on price and the two others, including "these guys," were not too far back. The money disparity with the leading suitor was significant enough to where it made sense to move forward with them. However, when we started to dig deeper into their offer, red flags began to appear, and their offer was shown to be somewhat weak in terms of credibility. We secretly listened in on many of the phone negotiations and discussions between this firm and our investment banker and we could really see their true colors. While they had been very nice and cordial to us in earlier meetings, their disposition and persona with the investment bankers was completely different. They appeared very arrogant, ruthless, and combative. We were taken back by this and concluded that we should factor this into our decision.

We would have to work with these people, and if we went through a rough patch, this is how they would be dealing with us. We wanted partners who understood the daily battle of business and who would understand the long-range perspective we had. Because the money was significant, we tried to like this firm . . . we really, really tried. But at the end of the day, we couldn't see ourselves working with these people, and despite the additional money, we gravitated toward the other suitors.

Ultimately, it was the two thirty-something guys we decided to go with, Clover Capital. Their proposal had several unique features, including the fact that they were raising money from high-net-worth individuals and weren't creating a classic venture fund with all its intricacies and complexities. The main factor influencing our decision was that we could see ourselves working with them and getting through difficult times. They also agreed to a tight timeline on closing. The last thing we wanted was for the deal to drag on for months, sapping our energy and producing stress.

On April 8, 2011, we closed our deal, selling 80 percent of the company. What a tremendous relief! Throughout the process, we assured them that we wanted to continue managing the business. We never really contemplated any other concept; it was important for us to make sure the business was on the right path. We just assumed that if we wanted to leave, we would start the process of installing new leadership and make the transition. So, the transition from Harvey and I owning 100 percent of the company to now collectively owning 20 percent of it was complete, but Clover Capital, which was owned by Alex Schneider and David Choe, wanted to get involved in our business. We certainly weren't against this, but we knew from past experience that this could go horribly wrong if it wasn't set up the right way and if they weren't the right partners.

Fortunately, we felt pretty good about the chemistry and concluded that they would be a good fit.

Nevertheless, the transition was an arduous one. I think everyone was protective of their turf. Gradually, we developed a framework for working together where everyone contributed. Alex and David are very smart businessmen, and they knew the bakery space well. They brought a lot of rigor to our management process and had contacts with key bakery technicians and other personnel that they had previously worked with. They also created the board of directors and brought in some savvy investors, including Bill Glastris and Mason Myers. Our circle of influence expanded nicely, and the "synergy" that everyone is always pursuing became evident. The whole experience was strengthening our business.

Over the next several months, Alex and David continually engaged us to learn more about the business and how they could help us grow. However, a few issues came up during the fall of 2011 that no one foresaw. Due to a drought across the country, many of our basic commodities such as sugar, flour, and soybean oil—things we didn't set contract pricing for—began to skyrocket. Consequently, we were forced to buy at higher prices and our margins tightened. It happened so quickly and forcefully that we were unable to raise customer pricing fast enough. Profits dropped dramatically.

The pressure was on instantly. It's never easy to raise customer prices, and this time was no exception. Every large customer was somewhat of a battle and a negotiation, and we found out who was reasonable and who wasn't, and which customers were in it for the long term. By the time the dust settled on commodities, we had taken a significant hit and had started to fail some loan covenants. To their credit, Alex and David didn't panic, and collectively, we all worked on a plan to get us back to a growth curve. They worked with the bank, who also took a long-term view of our plight and understood the ramifications of the downturn. Over the next several months, prices began to mitigate, and our profitability improved. Many of the price increases we instituted during the drought were maintained, and we started to see significant margin improvement. We were back on track.

In 2013, our sales exceeded $25 million. As the growth of the company stabilized again, Harvey and I started to think about building a team so we could eventually leave. We had mixed feelings, but deep in our hearts, we knew the time was coming. We just didn't know exactly when. We told the board, as well as Alex and David, our basic intentions, but we really couldn't give them a firm timeline. We knew that this was wishy-washy, but all we could tell them was that we wanted to leave at some point in the next few years, which left us time to get a team in place. We decided that we needed a chief operating officer (COO) to replace and supplement many of Harvey's efforts and a chief financial officer (CFO) to do the same for many of my duties. In the summer of 2014, we started this effort.

It was not an easy process. We tackled the COO position first and tried to summarize all the requirements, skill sets, and intangibles we wanted and needed. Did I mention the process wasn't easy? Replacing ourselves was never something we contemplated, but we gingerly plodded forward. I remember pondering the decision, wondering if we were making a mistake. But sooner or later, some crisis would develop and this decision would be confirmed. And then it would happen again.

If you see a poisonous spider, kill it . . . don't set up a focus group or a meeting to discuss it.

—STEVE MARKS

In the fall of 2014, Harvey met a candidate through a friend and thought they would be a good fit as the new COO. They met for breakfast a few times and things seem to click. Harvey felt that this person could be the answer. After several discussions, interviews, and lunches, we hired this person to be our new COO and moved in the direction of replacing Harvey. Did we make a mistake by not opening this position up to the rest of the world? We would eventually find out.

Shortly thereafter, we went through a lengthy process to hire a CFO who would eventually replace me. That process was much different. We involved dozens of employees so that we could get multiple opinions and real buy-in. We made sure that the candidate had the necessary skill sets in many different accounting functions. Ultimately, key staff made the decision based upon the interviews they conducted and the hard data about skill sets they had collected. After a few months, it seemed like our grand plan was working. Gradually, we took more off our plates and spoon-fed our proteges. It didn't hurt that we were doing well and that sales were increasing. We finished 2014 with another record year in sales and profits.

Once we sold the business, we began an annual tradition of having one of our four quarterly board meetings in Las Vegas. We reasoned that it was the most economical for everyone to fly into Las Vegas, coming from Ohio and California. Vegas also had available, inexpensive hotel rooms. Not so coincidentally, we orchestrated the meeting around Super Bowl weekend for added enjoyment.

For the February 2015 board meeting, we decided to invite other staff members, including the company's sales director, operations director, CFO, research and development director, and some of the sales staff. Oddly enough, many of them had never been to Las Vegas before, so I humbly showed them the ropes. The board had previously set up a 2014 bonus program for Harvey and me that involved four key components. As the bonus numbers were tallied for the year, we determined that we had only achieved three of the four criteria to get our full bonus. When I took a closer look at the calculations, there was an abnormality that stopped us from getting that fourth component. It really didn't make sense given our record year. Getting that fourth component would have resulted in a significant increase in the bonus for both Harvey and me.

I decided to call Dave Choe, who was mostly responsible for the development of the bonus, and state my position.

"It wasn't really fair," I told him. "We had a record year, and we should have gotten the maximum bonus."

After some back and forth, Dave said he understood my contention and would get back to me with a response. A few days went by before he called me back.

"The board has decided to give you the full bonus," he started. That was great news. "But we have a condition," he added.

"Uh oh," I thought, "What kind of condition?"

"When we go to Las Vegas," Dave continued, "we want you and Harvey to make a $1,000 bet at the roulette wheel on the number four to commemorate this gesture."

My mind was spinning. What kind of condition was this? Since the bonus was far greater than the thousand dollars we would be wagering, it was a very easy decision to make. I immediately chuckled, as did Dave, and we both started plotting the logistical measures on how the bet would take place. We decided that we would do it after the board dinner when everyone would be in a festive mood.

We held the meeting at Caesars Palace, one of the most iconic destinations in all of Las Vegas. As was typical, we started at 1:00 in the afternoon and worked until about 5:00. When things were going well, as was the case for the 2014 fiscal year, the subsequent board meeting was usually a lot more fun, productive, and jovial. This meeting was no exception. We ended the board meeting with instructions to meet for cocktails and dinner at a nice Italian restaurant within Caesars Palace. Harvey and I gathered our $1,000 in anticipation of our grand bet at the roulette wheel.

Over cocktails, one of our board members, Bill Glastris, took me aside and told me that it was foolish to make the $1,000 bet and to "just forget about it." Bill wasn't trying to circumvent the board decision; he was just trying to give good advice and it was a way for him to be able to kid around with Harvey and me. He loved every minute of it. I told Bill that we had a deal, and Harvey and I were ready to consummate it.

"It's a stupid bet . . . spend your money more productively," he protested.

Throughout cocktails and dinner, we bantered back and forth in a debate-like fashion, never getting to the point of agreeing on anything. Bill reluctantly acquiesced his position, and all of us left the restaurant in search of a roulette wheel in Caesars Palace.

Throughout our search, Bill kept chiding all of us for how ridiculous the venture was. The odds of winning a number on a roulette wheel are thirty-six to one and the payoff is thirty-five to one. So, if you bet $1,000 and win, you get your $1,000 back plus $35,000. All of us marched toward the gaming tables, clearly looking out of place, twelve mismatched executives and other overwhelmed staff members, all in tight formation, looking for a "stupid bet." We found a roulette wheel and huddled around, dominating the scene. I took out the $1,000 and tossed it to the croupier, the fancy French word for the person who spins the wheel. We were all smiling with anticipation.

"You can't bet that much here," said the croupier. "The limit is $200 on a number."

Bill took this moment to reinforce his argument.

"This is fate. We shouldn't be betting," he said.

I pulled back the money as we all watched the croupier spin the wheel with no risk on our part. We stuck around to see what would have happened.

"16 black!" proclaimed the croupier.

Whew . . . good thing we didn't bet!

Bill once again took this moment to say he had told us so.

As we started to walk away in search of our next venture, the croupier told us that if we wanted to bet the $1,000 on roulette, we could go the "high rollers room."

"Now we're talking!" I thought to myself. We all looked at each other and nodded in unison . . . except for Bill, who was steadfastly holding to his position. The high rollers room was a short 100 yards away, and we meandered in that direction.

After a short walk, we arrived there, unsure of whether or not to enter. The entrance infuses the notion that if you don't think you belong in the high rollers room, you don't. We all gingerly moved through the entrance and toward the roulette wheel. I promptly positioned the $1,000 on the table and we all moved into a circle around the wheel. Harvey and I ended up next to each other as we watched the croupier move a small figurine, evidencing our bet, to the number four.

Within seconds, the wheel was spinning, and we all watched with fervent expectation. I remember trying to fix my eyes on the number four, seeing the little ball continually pass by it. The wheel started to slow as it got close to revealing the winning number. I could see the ball momentarily land on four then bounce off it. Suddenly the wheel began to slow, and the ball landed firmly back on our placed bet—number four!

Almost unanimously, we all stood straight up, attempting to absorb the moment. There was a pause, and then we all let out a loud visceral scream that would have made the 1980 Miracle on Ice celebration seem mundane. Everyone within fifty yards looked in our direction like it was a traffic accident. High fives, hugs, and uncontrollable laughter filled the room as our frenzied celebration escalated. The loudest and wildest celebration came from none other than Bill Glastris.

Rather quickly, a small pile of chips was moved in my direction: a $25,000 chip, two $5,000 chips, and a $1,000 chip. I scooped them up before you could say "stupid bet" and pranced toward the casino cashier. The entourage followed. I scooted the chips to the cashier, ready for the payday.

"I am sorry, but I can't cash these chips," the cashier said.

"Why not?" I responded incredulously.

"For anything over $10,000, I have to talk to the crew manager first to verify this situation as you are not a regular customer," he responded.

Bill Glastris witnessed this exchange and moved in front of me, making sure he was heard by everyone within earshot. He looked back to the gamblers, away from the cashier:

"You mean to say, you win a bet . . . go to collect the bet . . . and now you won't pay the bet! No wonder Las Vegas is so successful . . . this is ridiculous," he snorted.

Harvey, who was over my other shoulder, watched this unfold and surreptitiously picked up the $25,000 chip, went back to the roulette wheel, and asked to get change. He was handed five $5,000 chips in exchange, and we quickly divvied up the spoils to five members of our support team. Each person swiftly cashed in the chips and handed the money back to me, just as Bill Glastris had ended his diatribe on the evils of Vegas betting. I had $36,000 in hundred-dollar bills, and we were off to the bar to recount every single millisecond and detail of our experience. It was a glorious few moments that none of us will ever forget.

Fortunately, there was no shortage of bars at Caesars Palace, and we rapidly bellied up to one as everyone ordered. David Choe came up to me and put his arm over my shoulder.

"Pretty good bet, huh?"

We laughed for a moment. What was never discussed nor ever considered was the question of who the money belonged to. My "favorite" argument was that the money belonged to Harvey and me because it was our money that funded the bet. The other, less beloved position is that there was a trade for us getting the bonus and that the money belonged to the company. I won't reveal the exact details of how we resolved this conundrum, but the first day we arrived back to the plant, we walked up to each office and management team member to hand them a nice stack of bills to spend on whatever they wanted.

Monty Hall, rest in peace, would have been proud. Bill Glastris, very much alive, still shows his pride when he relays his version of the story to anyone who will listen.

In 2015, sales surpassed $30 million for the first time. We also began to look more closely at our enterprise resource planning (ERP) system, or, as academics would better describe it, "an integrated business management software designed to manage the business efficiently and seamlessly." Entrepreneurs describe it as something you have to almost die to figure out, spending an inordinate amount of time implementing it only to find out that it isn't working nearly as well as everyone told you it would. Bottom line: we determined we needed a new and better system to accomplish the food industry's many regulatory requirements.

We told our board that we wanted to start the process of purchasing a new ERP system. For those of you reading this who are thinking about how you installed a new ERP system, coming in below costs and having everything work out brilliantly, I suggest you ask others in your organization about their recollections. Yours is inaccurate. We spent a few months researching the best ERP system for our company, interviewing and narrowing down the list to just a few candidates. We wanted to see firsthand how the systems would work, make several site visits, and take some "test drives." We finally felt we had our choice of an ERP system to move forward. We discussed this need to the board and a loose timeline was put in place.

We also realized we were busting at the seams and rapidly running out of capacity. It was becoming increasingly difficult to produce in our facility. We were out of production space as well as freezer and storage space. We were continually navigating buying decisions, balancing how much space we had and the possibility of making good financial decisions. We realized that to grow, we needed to expand again.

We started the ugly and exhausting process to determine and justify how, why, and when we would implement a major expansion to our facility. We were renting outside storage space and the cost and inefficiency was eating at us. We moved very quickly to assemble a plan, selecting a builder and holding discussions with our board and banker. To do what we wanted to, the costs (in excess of $5 million) started to look problematic. We were only adding about 15,000 square feet. You could probably buy a 50,000 square-foot facility for the same costs we were contemplating. Could we really justify it? Most of our expenditures were for reformatting the facility, expanding throughput, and increasing our flexibility and overall capacity.

It was a struggle to convince everyone that spending this kind of money was the best course of action. We also wanted to start the implementation of the new ERP system at the same time. Yes, you read that sentence accurately . . . we wanted to implement a new ERP system while simultaneously undertaking a major plant expansion and renovation. Many board discussions ensued.

Our argument, or rather Harvey's argument, was that it was more efficient to birth twins then to have one kid after the other. (If you are a woman reading this, I am sorry.) Despite having six kids between Harvey and me, the two of us had no recollection of personally feeling any pain during the births. That was our basis and fundamental thesis. Although there was wise counsel against the concept of doing both, the board reluctantly sanctioned our approach and we delved into the unpleasant process. As it turned out, convincing everyone was the easy part. In all our board meetings, Harvey and I were never too proud or afraid to let everyone know our true feelings. Actively engaging and listening to this support provided needed comfort to us, guidance to fuel better solutions and make our company better.

While we moved forward with the ERP system, we started construction in 2016, planning to add more freezer space and eliminate outside storage, to reconfigure the warehouse areas to production space, and to add new warehouse space. We developed teams of employees to look over our plans and figure out the best way to configure the flow and layout. Many changes were being made and we continued to feel good about our decision. But there were unforeseen problems that dogged us. The first hurdle became the soil we were excavating. Apparently, it wasn't solid enough to support a building foundation or driveways, which caused significant costs to replace it so it would allow for construction. Our fire suppression system, a system to transport water from one point to another through a sprinkler system, also wasn't designed adequately and robustly enough.

No one took responsibility for these issues, and the blame game created a quagmire with no recourse but to bite the bullet and add significant costs to the project. Our initial estimates proved too optimistic, and the project quickly and effortlessly spiraled into total costs that fueled a daily dose of antacid. It was difficult enough to justify the costs when we had first started, but with the added overruns, even more pressure was added to the mix. Banker and board conversations were frequent and lengthy.

My daily battle with stress was beginning to take its toll, and I was continually looking for solutions to ease the strain. I had read and learned enough to know that I needed to build an infrastructure of balance and health. I understood that people who do not have balance in their life and are unhealthy cannot successfully weather the storms of adversity. Smart entrepreneurs build a personal, balanced infrastructure of exercise, rest, and mental health. This approach was a constant theme in my life and something I would continually strive to achieve. Sometimes I was successful, and sometimes I fell a bit short. But I wasn't giving up.

Having to eat bakery products every day (and sometimes nights) had me incorporating fitness into my lifestyle. Exercising, usually five to six days a week, was very therapeutic for me and certainly good for the stress. I had added mediation a few years before the new construction began and was trying to utilize that as well. I have also run a number of marathons and other long-distance races. All of this helped me immeasurably, and I am very thankful that I had the fortitude to keep it all up.

I once stumbled upon another interesting concept when I read a legendary story about a contest between two lumberjacks. The first man in the contest was your stereotypical lumberjack; young, muscle-bound, bearded, clad in plaid, and weighing in at 250 pounds and standing six feet, five inches tall. The second lumberjack was new to the field. He was young, only five feet, eight inches tall, and he weighed 150 pounds dripping wet. They both had identical equipment and techniques.

The rules of the competition were straightforward. Each man would have four hours to chop down as much lumber as possible. Whoever had the most cut lumber at the conclusion of that time would be the victor. The whole village gathered to watch the seemingly lopsided competition.

The contest began right at noon. The first lumberjack, the conventional one, aggressively chopped with a skillful, precise technique and pace while never losing velocity. He was strong and consistent. The crowd marveled at his level of effort and the demonstration of his strength. The second lumberjack also had excellent technique and effort, and he chopped away with the same enthusiasm and drive. However, every forty-five minutes or so he would stop, go into his cabin for ten minutes, and then return to start chopping again.

At the conclusion of the four hours, the officials tallied each lumberjack's amount. To everyone's astonishment, the smaller, younger lumberjack had amassed more lumber and was proclaimed the victor. Many members of the crowd approached him, wondering how it was possible. What was his secret? What did he do during those ten-minute breaks?

Now here is the twist in my story. As this story typically goes, the young lumberjack replies, "I was sharpening my ax." And the crowd goes crazy.

While that is a great story and it holds a valuable lesson, I feel that in this day and age, the ending would be more appropriate if he had said, "I was napping."

Napping, to me, was a way to mentally sharpen my abilities for what was to follow. After reading this story, I started to incorporate a nap, a scientific nap if you will, into my daily work routine. When I first began napping, I felt some guilt. I wasn't sure where it was really coming from because I had always worked hard at my job. Perhaps I was thinking that the time I spent working would be more beneficial than "secretly" snoozing in my office.

Over time, I refined the process, experimenting with various techniques and processes to arrive at the perfect nap. I tried different parts of the day and different methods of waking myself up. I eventually learned that taking a twenty-three-minute nap after lunch allowed me to wake up invigorated and to work the remaining hours of the workday with a productive energy that I usually lacked in the afternoon. No, I am not ashamed. I am a proud napper, and I continuously recommend it to anyone who wants to sharpen their ax.

Our ERP project was in full swing. Several teams were working to start its implementation. It was very hard for everyone to remain focused on normal daily activities while also tackling the ERP and construction projects.

During the summer of 2016, we also faced a calamity that almost crippled us and increased my personal need for an exit plan. On a hot Sunday in July, we had a rainstorm with significant winds that rocked and soaked the area in a very short time. Unbeknownst to us, the contractor had been working on an extension of the machine room (basically the central nervous system of our plant that housed all the critical components that control the freezer and other important sectors). The contractor had taken off the roof of the existing machine room to allow for one single roof to cover both the old and extended areas. They had used a flimsy tarp to cover the area, and it was no match for the epic storm that barreled through the area. The machine room was exposed, and rain cascaded into this vital area, eventually causing the freezer system to malfunction and shut down. When someone asked me what kept me up at night, the freezer system was always on my list. It housed millions of dollars of inventory and if it faltered and stayed out of commission for more than twenty-four hours, we could have been out of business.

We didn't have a backup generator and we were always vulnerable to this possibility. Fortunately, in the more than thirty years prior to this, we had managed to dodge the inevitable bullets that were fired at us by figuring out, scrambling, or begging the utility company or repair companies to come to our aid. And up until this point in time, we had been successful. But this situation was unlike anything we had ever seen. Water filled the room to knee-high levels, and it was unclear what could be done to get things repaired. The clock was ticking . . . we basically had twenty-four hours if we kept all the freezer doors shut. The rainstorm had occurred around 3:00 p.m. that afternoon. By 5:00 p.m., Harvey had been notified and began to assemble the team to solve the crisis. Our ammonia freezer vendor was contacted with an emergency call to get people up to our plant to assess the damage and figure out what we needed to do.

Contingency plans were in place to bring in trucking companies to move the inventory to an off-site warehouse. All the production teams were shut down for the foreseeable future. Harvey would be staying on site until there was a resolution. I met him at the plant in the evening and we both lamented how bad it looked and wondered if we could recover from it. I remember looking at him and jokingly remarking, "It was a good run." We both could only muster a brief smile.

Overnight, many good and bad ideas were kicked around with Harvey, our maintenance staff, and the ammonia freezer vendor. One thing that became crystalized for me was that I wanted to exit the company. I simply didn't want the stress and responsibility anymore, and I knew that as I got older, my priorities were shifting, primarily to my family. The only viable way to finally make the shift completely would be to sell the business. But that would be a separate and significant endeavor only if we could get through this calamity in one piece. Our maintenance crew and the freezer vendors worked throughout the night. Pumping systems were brought in to remove standing water.

Basically, the system had been shut down by a fried compressor. Fortunately, we had three of them and the other two were not damaged. But the storm had caused the ammonia to be displaced in the system. Without ammonia circulating to the right areas, the system wouldn't run. The team came up with a way, albeit a very risky one, to move the ammonia through the system and to try and get it running again. By "risky," I mean a potential explosion and/or complete damage to the system was, in the words of Tom Clancy, a "clear and present danger."

To even attempt this fix would take several hours, and we were running out of time. At midnight, we made the decision to start the process. When the vendor triggered the switch with no initial repercussions, we all felt encouraged that we had found a potential solution. At 8:00 a.m., the final element of the plan was put in place and to our astonishment, the system started up again. Within five hours, the freezer temperature had returned to near zero. We had escaped business failure. Our collective sigh of relief could be heard for miles.

Later that summer, other production problems began to surface. We were shipping orders later and later as well as shorting customers. Fortunately, our system could tell us this rather quickly and we tried to react . . . rather, we put this task on our new COO. He assured us that he could and would handle the issue. More and more cracks began to show as our COO tried to solve the problem. He simply couldn't get his hands around it and tried to throw more and more labor at it. Our key labor indicator shot up, sending out all kinds of warning signs. After several months of watching this unfold, it became apparent that we needed to do something very bold.

One morning, Harvey told me that he thought our COO would need to be let go and that he would have to immerse himself back into the game. We didn't wait long. We told our board and made the move in September of 2016. Firing someone is never easy (well, sometimes it is, but rarely), but this was especially difficult, given that we liked and cared about this individual. Harvey gave him the news, and we made plans for Harvey to assume his previous role. Meanwhile, my replacement seemed to be working well. I gave up more and more each day. I could see my exit plans unfolding.

The storm episode motivated me to push hard for everyone to be on the divestiture bandwagon. At the February 2017 board meeting, a spirited debate and discussion took place about the mechanics and timing of such a purposeful undertaking. We looked at 2017 as a pivotal year for getting many things accomplished, including making headway on our construction projects and getting closer to launching the ERP system. David and Alex talked to investment bankers, putting out feelers on selling the business. The general consensus was that Main Street Gourmet would be an attractive acquisition for a multitude of acquirers. However, we kept hearing the same drumbeat of negative factors. We didn't yet have added capacity, and the completion and final cost of construction was still up in the air. Our ERP system hadn't launched yet, and it was unclear what kind of mishaps might still evolve.

In June of 2018, we finally launched our new, expensive ERP system. As everyone we had previously talked with promised, it was a colossal headache. It was all-hands-on-deck, and we muddled through every month by learning the system ever so slowly. While we started to have regrets, we realized that there was no turning back. Day by day, we made headway and became encouraged that a time would come where we would have confidence in the system.

Throughout 2018, David and Alex continued to meet with prospective acquirers, and we brought a few of them into the plant for a visit. Most of their questions revolved around the completion of the ERP system and the construction. It became increasingly clear that we wouldn't be able to sell the business until both issues were settled. Further complicating their interest was the fact that we couldn't take on more business and that our growth was becoming flat. Trying to explain the circumstances by saying that we had to turn down opportunities once we'd reached our capacity made us look vulnerable. Even though it was the truth, our comments sounded hollow and whiny. As we grinded through 2018, more and more of the construction was completed and we took on more opportunities. Our sales force was told to open the spigots and everyone became more open-minded. Gradually, sales began to grow again.

....

Muffin Recipe #6:
Ability to Overcome Adversity

INGREDIENTS AND DIRECTIONS:
Realize that adversity will always be present

Build an infrastructure of balance and health

Involve and communicate with your colleagues, advisors, and family

Practice being an optimist

BAKING AND PREP TIME:
These situations will never go away

THE DECISION

**It's ok to enjoy your success,
just don't quite believe it.**

—STEVE MARKS

I understood that I had reached a decision point and that I did not want to push the business to that next level. I was honest with myself and knew what direction was necessary. I also knew that I was limited and unable to keep up with the same enthusiasm and passion that I was typically accustomed to. I understood that I was good at some things and not so good at others. Harvey was in the same boat. We were able to leverage each other's strengths and weaknesses for the benefit of the company. We also brought in key individuals to fill in the many gaps our weaknesses created. This was one of the principles and secret sauces that fueled our success and enabled us to be great partners.

At our February 2019 board meeting, everyone agreed that we would put the business up for sale. Timing would still be crucial as we had to show growth that year. Most of the unknowns were behind us and the future looked bright. The plan was to hold discussions with three to five investment bankers with a target date of June for starting the process. We would open the door and put the book together that would advertise to the world that we were selling. We were still hopeful that someone would step up and make us an offer that would derail the normal process and avoid all the disruption that comes with it. As sort of a test suggested by Harvey, I moved to part-time hours to see how both the company and I would adjust to my limited involvement. I liked it.

In June, we were just about to bring in some key investment bankers for interviews when two private equity firms emerged, wanting to put some preliminary offers together. Alex and Dave did their magic and created a mini competitive bidding process. After visits from both companies, we became excited and increasingly convinced that we could avoid a long, drawn-out process. Initial bids were received in June and both were fairly close.

Our choice about who to sell to also became very difficult because both candidates were great organizations. Finally, Shore Capital Partners emerged as both the highest bidder and the best partner. They understood that Harvey would agree to stay on for one to two years for an orderly transition while I would retire.

On July 15, we signed a letter of intent to sell the company with a closing date of August 31, 2019. It was a very short timeline but an encouraging one; it was a signal that the buyers would put in the resources to make the deal happen and happen quickly. The more time there was to close, the more time there was for things to potentially fall apart. Shore Capital Partners, headed by a fast-talking yet charismatic founder, Justin Ishbia, seemed to push all the right buttons in both pursuing us and in finalizing the deal with Alex and David. His company had quite an impressive track record in the medical field, and now they wanted to do the same with a food platform.

Teams of legal, accounting, environmental, human resource, and food operations descended upon our company. It seemed no stone was left unturned. I am pretty sure I had to turn over my 23andMe password at one point. Either I didn't remember the other times we had sold, or perhaps it was because there was so much at stake for Shore, but the diligence investigations seemed excessive. It felt like we were answering the same types of questions over and over, in some cases going back many years to discuss an issue. I remember one senior member of the accounting team who was suspicious about "why was our accounts receivable were aging so good." Damned if you do, damned if you don't.

August 31 was getting closer and closer, and it looked like that might be the date. I was getting very little sleep each night. My brain was rifling through all the remaining issues and contemplating what life after the deal would look like. In our minds, all it would have taken was one large customer account discontinuing a product to cancel the whole deal. About ten days before closing, we got a call from our testing laboratory, indicating that one of their swabs on our equipment had tested positive for listeria. If the freezer going down was a nine on anxiety scale, finding a dangerous pathogen was off the charts. End of deal. Maybe the end of the company. Throughout the day, as we were going through all the scenarios of recalls, cause, and blame, we got another call from the laboratory. It was a mistake . . . something they called a "false positive." I called it taking ten years off my life.

On August 24, a week before the scheduled closing date, Shore told us we needed to push the closing back to September 6 because the legal team needed more time to work through the agreements. When your mind is set on a date and you are thinking about it over and over and then suddenly the date changes, it's an emotional roller coaster that is hard to recover from. And I hate traditional roller coasters anyway. Everyone was saying the right things, but it didn't matter. We were on pins and needles. On September 5, the night before the closing, there was even more stress—lightning struck our compressor, knocking out our freezer and burning a critical part of it.

Was this a dream? A sign for someone above? More importantly, would we have the replacement part on the premises, or would we need to scramble like we did in the summer of 2016? It was an obscure piece to replace, but miraculously . . . drumroll . . . wait for it . . . we had a back-up! *Touchdown! Home Run!* The same night of the lightning strike, Shore called us again and wanted to move the closing to Monday, September 9. All indications were that we could close on September 9. But on a late evening call with the attorneys on Sunday, September 8, it got changed to September 16.

I could feel my hair getting grayer by the minute. The next week dragged on. I was afraid to look at my emails in the morning for fear that something would derail the closing again. On Sunday, September 15, I went to sleep early in the hopes of avoiding any issues. I woke up the next morning around 5:00 a.m. and reached over for my cell phone, not sure what to expect. The subject of an email from Alex read, "All Systems Go."

A sense of relief filled my brain and body, but as they say, it's not over till it's over. I got to work that morning with guarded optimism. I checked email right away and saw no indication that we wouldn't close. I looked at my bank app to see if the money had somehow gotten there early. No chance. Throughout the morning, I periodically checked but knew I would have to wait. Finally, at 1:07 p.m., the money had been received in my bank account. I took a screenshot right away for fear it would disappear.

I looked at Harvey—our offices had always been next to one another with a door between them—and we both knew we had reached the finish line. A thirty-two-year partnership was nearing its finality. Nothing was said, but we both had smiles on our faces that Stevie Wonder could have read. It was an indescribable magical feeling, yet it was a little anticlimactic because I had been thinking about it and predicting how I would feel. It's never how you expect it to be.

Congratulatory emails flooded in from our board and the Shore team. I sent the screenshot of the bank account to my wife, Jeannine, who asked if it was her share. I was elated but didn't really let out any emotion. Harvey and I decided to celebrate at a local hangout with two close friends. I got in my car, and as I was leaving the plant, it all hit me, and I let out a scream that would strain my voice for the next two days. It was a cathartic scream that hit just the right note. I struggled to find a song on the radio that would capture the moment and give my journey more meaning. I kept finding love songs. I am sorry, but an Ambrosia song was just not what I was looking for. I finally found a Springsteen song . . . "Thunder Road." I screamed every word. Thank god I was alone.

After the closing, I called my dad to tell him the news, and I could feel his pride as he congratulated me with accolades and warm wishes. That was another feeling that will be hard to forget. I pulled into Gasoline Alley, a local joint with great beers and a vibe that was perfect for the celebration. Harvey and I and our close friends recounted every detail we could recall about the last several days. Every few minutes, I would let out a noticeable sigh, knowing of our accomplishments. I didn't care . . . it was too good a feeling. While we were there, we received a few phone calls from more friends who had heard the news. It was just right. After two beers, we departed to our homes to extend the jubilation.

I walked into the house in a great mood fueled by two beers and the success of a hard- fought sale. My wife, Jeannine, greeted me, and we hugged. She knew what this meant to me and could feel the moment's importance. I couldn't stop smiling as we moved to our deck and I recounted the last several days, knowing she had already heard most of the drama. She patiently listened and chimed in, encouraging me to keep the conversation going. I kept repeating many of the same situations, problems, and dilemmas, creating different spins and analysis. They were stories she no doubt had heard over and over, but it didn't matter to her.

It was a great day, and later, as I got into bed, I pondered all that had been accomplished over the last several weeks, months, and years. It was an amazing feeling, with little regret and only the future to determine. Leading up to the sale, I purposely refused to determine what I was going to do after the sale for fear I would jinx it. Now my brain was flooded with those questions, but not with the typical anxiety that one might expect to accompany them. I had a blank slate and could move in many different directions. For now, though, I let the journey just sink in and I slowly drifted into a euphoric sleep.

Shore didn't waste much time setting up systems and incorporating a "100-day plan." No more daydreaming for me . . . back to work! They drop-shipped a slew of hot-shot financial staffers whose job was to integrate every company they purchased into a cohesive system, which allowed for and promoted better reporting, best practices, and the ability to solve any problem they encountered. Our staff was not used to this type of scrutiny and upheaval, but they did whatever it took. We could see the layers of bureaucracy starting to build. While this was not our style, we understood we were in a new reality and picked very few spots to push back.

While this was going on, I got a call from our new "boss," wanting to discuss my impending retirement. By the way, as an entrepreneur, the word "boss" is pretty much a dirty word. When you have worked most of your adult life without one (enter your wife or husband joke here) and you learn that you suddenly have one, it forces you to take on a new perspective that's difficult to manage. Leading up to this process, I had always proclaimed my retirement date would be at the end of the year, which would give me some time to transfer a lot of knowledge, create an orderly transition, and ease into retirement life. For some reason, the Shore team thought I would be leaving within a few weeks. You can imagine the shock when I heard this, and anxiety rippled through my body. I was certainly willing to move on, but a few weeks seemed very sudden for me. It was something I hadn't envisioned. I explained that I was always planning on leaving at the end of the year and that leaving sooner than that was not something I wanted to do, let alone orchestrate.

They had put in motion a lot of planning and budgeting around my departure in a few weeks and that's what they expected. We compromised that I would depart on October 31 . . . about forty-five days away. While this wasn't ideal, I could deal with it, and my mind started to go through the transition gyrations. I started the process of telling those people the transition would affect the most, and I began to plan out how it would evolve. I started to contemplate what things to take with me, what to throw away, and what relics to leave: old coffee and travel mugs, stupid trophies (a third-place trophy from our annual chili competition would reluctantly be flaunted), celebratory wine bottles I never opened (I am pretty sure a 1991 Pinot Noir bought at the 7-Eleven wouldn't be any good), old cell phones and chargers, rulers, tape measures, hand sanitizers in a myriad of weird containers, and on and on.

It was part fun, part sentimental, and part ugly. I put together a "moving sale," commandeering a large conference table to display all the things most people would call junk. As I completed this display, people started to congregate around the area, asking me what was going on. It was a "moving sale" and everything was "free," I explained. That's all I needed to say. Word spread throughout the plant and dozens of coworkers came out of the woodwork for this once-in-a-career, everything-must-go sale. Over the next several days, I replenished the display as I continued cleaning out my office. People started to anticipate my offerings, hovering around my office and wondering what I would come out with next. It's true that one man's junk is another man's treasure. Eventually, I started to run out of nuggets and my looming departure truly started to sink in.

Finally, October 31 arrived. I packed my last box to take home. I was feeling a little uneasy about the awkwardness of walking out of the building. I sort of envisioned the scene in *Dead Poets Society* (I encourage you to google it if you haven't seen it) when the students stand on their desks and proclaim "O Captain! My Captain!" to Robin Williams's character to show their respect and admiration. That wasn't going to happen here. A few clumsy hugs and handshakes came my way as I moved toward the exit, mumbling "Thank you" over and over. Before getting in my car, I looked back at the plant with an odd feeling. It was the same feeling you got on the last day of grade school . . . happy for summer, but sad that you wouldn't see the same people as frequently anymore.

Despite the typical mayhem that comes with any transition, the company hummed along and went on to have record sales and profits for the year. It was exactly the scenario we had hoped for. Strong sales and profits solve a lot of problems and calm a lot of concerns. Harvey was becoming immersed in the new setup and, even though he didn't want significant changes to the business, seemed to be content in his sole CEO role. Harvey and I had always been co-CEOs and had always had the mindset that we wouldn't do something that the other wouldn't buy into.

Now, Harvey had new partners, a new structure, and a new protocol he had to navigate. The company had its first board meeting in December. As part of my exit, Shore and I had agreed that I would stay on as a board member. I was happy for that as it would provide a good way for me to stay involved. Shore had enlisted a cadre of independent board members as well. These were high-level individuals who were generally working at well-established food organizations. They had been through many different growth cycles and had seen almost every kind of twist and turn a business could enjoy and endure. Harvey and Alex were also board members. Shore also had three individuals on the board. Included in the meeting were five or so Main Street Gourmet employees as well as several Shore team members who acted as observers. Overall, we had about twenty-some people in our conference room that was built to accommodate ten. It was like Thanksgiving dinner as we utilized extra mismatched chairs, aligning them in odd configurations to adjust for this overcapacity. I felt as though I was sitting at the kids' table because I wasn't used to not having control. It was not the kind of scenario Harvey and I would have put together, but we understood the new reality. Shore had the right to do it their way.

As 2019 came to a close and the hundred-day plan was completed, I felt as though the transition was somewhat complete. Shore had identified ten or so acquisition targets and had hired someone to implement their strategy. They had also brought in a CEO to oversee the overall food platform. Harvey and I didn't talk as much during this time. I was a little reluctant to ask too much about the business other than how it was going. Harvey had agreed to stay on when we had first developed the strategy to sell, and I could tell he was second-guessing that decision. It was especially hard when he would drop mail off at my house on his way to work and had to see me in sweatpants, drinking a cup of coffee. Of course, I had no choice but to milk it a little and played up the carefree life of a retiree. He would have done the same. I would go back inside to have a relaxing day while he went on to work to navigate the business landscape and the new establishment that we had brought on ourselves.

We certainly had no regrets, and the entrepreneurial lesson on timing I included earlier in this book had significant meaning as the dire events and circumstances of early 2020 unfolded. What would have happened if we had tried to sell the business six months later? I know that answer. I know the ramifications of our fortuitous timing and luck. I try not to work myself up too much about what things would have looked like. I know that sometimes, the luck goes in your favor, especially if you work hard enough.

I know and understand how fortunate I have been. I was able to follow my dream, build a wonderful business with my best friend, and meet so many great people while building lifelong friendships. Many people don't get to follow their passions as they circumnavigate life's choices and circumstances. Ever since I was a kid, I wanted to start a business that could flourish and be my life's work. What I didn't realize, or ever contemplate, was how big of an impact this desire and choice would have on my life, pride, and satisfaction. I also didn't realize how many other lives would be impacted, how many careers would be created, and how many individuals would thrive as well. It's incredibly rewarding to see so many people generate a foundation of wealth and success because of something we started and cultivated.

I am very proud of the achievements of the Akron Marathon. We have been true to our original mission statement and we've accomplished many of our original goals. We have been selected as one of the top fifty marathons and the largest five-person marathon relay in the US. We've raised millions of dollars for local charitable organizations and provided an annual economic impact to the community of more than $8 million. It has been a daunting effort but one that has been very satisfying and rewarding. One person said to me that they thought we started the marathon so people could eat more muffins.

Ultimately, it's those kinds of circumstances and accomplishments that are so gratifying to me after a long and varied business career. I often look back and wonder if we made the right moves at the right time, and what paths we could have gone down if different decisions been made. Some seemingly bad decisions have turned out to ultimately be good ones and vice versa. Much of what I have recounted has been serendipitous. Some would call it just plain dumb luck. That doesn't bother me. I know that the road to success is never easy and that there are many detours, rest stops, and breakdowns along the way. The start of my entrepreneurial journey began with these cherished words: "Going once, going twice . . . sold to the twenty-six-year-old nerd in the back of the room." I am so thankful for that day, and the portal it opened up, allowing me to follow a dream in this great game we call business.

....

Muffin Recipe #7:
Know Thyself

INGREDIENTS AND DIRECTIONS:
Be honest about your limitations, capabilities, and aspirations

Be ambitious and relentless in the pursuit of your goals

Take initiative and act decisively

Engage others to be passionate about the quest

BAKING AND PREP TIME:
A lifetime

FINAL WORDS

There is an age-old question that frequently comes up in business journals and college classrooms: Are entrepreneurs born or made? It's essentially the business version of the chicken or the egg question.

The question is impossible to answer with either one of the options. Invariably, an attempt at answering it usually involves a process of subjective analysis. I have no definitive answer either. I feel that being an entrepreneur requires certain innate traits as well as a lot of life experience that shapes one's desires, risk tolerance, ambitions, and passion. We shouldn't ignore the circumstances of good fortune of an individual whose road was paved with ample privilege and opportunity, either. A certain president, for example, recounted his ability to get into business by starting off "with a small loan of a million dollars from my father." (The question of whether this individual is actually an entrepreneur is also up for debate.) We also shouldn't ignore the many socioeconomic roadblocks, as well as the discrimination and racism, that reduce the chances for some people to become entrepreneurs, let alone successful ones. However, I think a better analysis of the question would start by focusing on the traits inherent in successful entrepreneurs.

I think an entrepreneur is born with certain valuable traits and intelligence, with the balance being a matter of one's life experiences. It would be very hard to break down the ratio of born traits to life experiences. I see a lot of people who want to be entrepreneurs who may have the means to start a business, but they just don't have the necessary elements to make it happen and thrive.

So, what are the necessary traits to be a successful entrepreneur? Within this book, I have tried to identify some principles that an entrepreneur must understand, embrace, and utilize within the game of business. But what about the inherent traits of an entrepreneur?

Again, you'll get a lot of different and varied answers. But to me, they need to include some basics. A successful entrepreneur:

- Is a risk-taker—one who is not intimidated by taking calculated risks
- Has a certain confidence (and maybe even a bit of arrogance)
- Is ambitious and relentless in pursuit of their goals
- Takes initiative and acts decisively
- Embodies a life force of independence
- Has the ability to engage others to be passionate about the quest

Keep in mind that merely having these abilities doesn't guarantee success—that's a whole different analysis.

There are also many entrepreneurs who have taken different paths within the entrepreneurial sector. For example, are you the type of person who is a natural franchisor, a trailblazer who can originate the concept for a large restaurant chain? Or would you rather be the franchisee type, the person who takes the restaurant concept and expands it within a region while setting up your own network? Both are entrepreneurs, yet they're very different. What is appealing to one person may be disdained by others. Personally, I feel I can only be the franchisor—the person developing the concept, setting up the rules, and controlling more of the game. Others would rather know the rules up front, limit the downside, and have a better picture of the game.

Your path can be determined by looking inward and being honest with yourself. Many people are pushed into being entrepreneurs because of outside influences and circumstances that aren't necessarily under their control: downsizing, layoffs, or simply being fired. There are many successful entrepreneurs who were reluctantly cast into vocations that they never really aspired to before because of these kinds of circumstances and who went on to create great companies. Thomas Edison and Walt Disney are prime examples.

Prototypical professions have valuable perks, safety, and security. Not everyone is cut out for the entrepreneurial lifestyle. I am not saying that one is better than the other. What is important to know are what traits or philosophical views you gravitate toward.

Which jobs thrilled you and which ones were a disappointment? Did you like coaching the team or were you happier getting directions for how to make the play? Is one bird in the hand really better than potentially two in the bush? Do you really want all the responsibility, or do you not want to be burdened by work once the clock hits 5:00 p.m.? I think my destiny was sealed when I embarked on selling cinnamon toothpicks back in the fourth grade.

As an entrepreneur, I can tell you that my work life has stayed close to me, even when I was home and on vacation. It's not always something I am proud of, but it's something I couldn't help but do. Ask yourself some hard-hitting questions and you'll know and understand yourself better and be able to plot a truer course for your life.

I hope this book's stories and lessons have given you some insight and understanding into entrepreneurship. If you are trying to understand and decide whether you should be jumping into this world, I hope my insights will help you as you contemplate. If you are already an entrepreneur, I hope it has provided you with some ideas, concepts, and revelations, and that perhaps it's even motivated you to be a better entrepreneur. That's all I can ask for.

AFTERWORD

Of all the calamities I've ruminated over, or moments when I morphed something insignificant into something grandiose (and believe me there were many), a global pandemic was not something on my radar. People would always need food, and Main Street Gourmet would always be able to fill that need, I reasoned. But as most of the restaurants in the US ceased their dine-in operations in early 2020, the company's business was sliced in half almost overnight.

The other portion of the company's business was supermarkets, so that business was somewhat stable. Still, the company had to furlough about half its workforce, which was incredibly painful to watch or hear about, even if I was not involved anymore. Many hard decisions on who should be essential and who should be furloughed had to be made by Harvey and his team. Complicating those decisions was the fact that Harvey knew the personal situations of so many employees and couldn't avoid factoring those elements into his decisions. The company went into crisis mode, trying to preserve cash for what would likely become several weeks or months before any kind of normalcy returned.

Vendor and customer conversations dominated the day and tactics changed by the hour. All plans for acquisition were on hold and all of the ambitious plans about strategy and synergies with the Shore portfolio were pushed aside. Would the company survive or be reduced to some fraction of its former self? We always had hope in our mindset and a clear plan for success. Never in our history did we have to ponder or analyze the worst-case scenario with murky vision. Still, Main Street Gourmet was lucky compared to so many businesses that had no activity or infrastructure to rely upon. As I write this, we are still in the throngs of this evil pandemic. However, I don't hesitate at all to proclaim that the company's resiliency will win the day and that it will emerge ready to tackle the next challenge.